I0799619

Dedication

This book is dedicated to all the women who today love their jobs, who have the great opportunity to use their talents, education, experiences, strengths, and leadership skills to own companies and provide not only a living for their families but jobs for others, and women who work in corporations, who lead, train, develop, and mentor other women to be better today than they were yesterday.

This book is dedicated to all the women of tomorrow. I want you to know the sky's the limit. You can be whatever you want to be, but know with that comes hard work, education, mentors, and the desire to make a difference in your life and others.

I love that we can be whatever it is we want to be.

I love that we live in a time and a place where if you can dream it, you can do it.

Thank you to all of you who take the time to read my book; may it help each of you in some way to be better today than you were yesterday.

Tell me, what is it you plan to do with your one wild and precious life?

— Mary Oliver

Acknowledgments

Writing this book has been an awesome experience. When we help others succeed, we are blessed more than they are. I wrote this book to help women whom I may never meet in person. I hope my experiences can help you, my reader, succeed at whatever your passion is.

My first "Thank You" is to my Lord and Savior; with Him all things are possible.

My biggest blessing in life is my son, Matthew. I love being his mom; having him in my life has made me strive to be a better person and someone he can look up to. I am so proud of you, Matthew; you are the best.

Thank you to my sister, Nancy, who is one of my biggest fans and my dear friends, for believing in me, encouraging me, praying for me, and always loving me.

Thank you to my dear, sweet, and loving friend Carmella. The trials in your life have made you stronger, the years have made you wiser, the love of your wonderful husband has made you softer, and your love of God has made you everything you've ever wanted to be. I am so proud of you and of the life you live. May we all find our place in life; I'll never forget when you said to me, "I finally know where I belong." Our friendship has endured the test of time—and I feel blessed to be your friend. You will have my love and prayers always.

A big thank you to someone who at one time was my boss and now is my dear friend, Ron. You believed in my abilities and saw my potential when I was just starting in the restaurant industry. You have been and will always be my friend and someone who believes in me no matter what. I cherish our friendship, and I appreciate that you let me bounce ideas off of you and always give me your unbiased opinion. Thank you for your encouragement. Like me, you believe all things are possible.

Thank you to David Montanaro and Harry Roberts. The opportunity to be here at Pallino is truly a blessing.

Thank you to Patrick Snow—without his knowledge, his enthusiasm, and his professionalism, this journey would not have been so enjoyable. If you are interested in writing or speaking, I highly recommend you contact Patrick. He is so professional and knowledgeable and a pleasure to work with.

Contents

Introduction

When I was thirteen years old, I started working at the fast food restaurant my mom owned. Today, I enjoy being the chief operations officer (COO) of a restaurant company in the Northwest. There is not a job in the restaurant business I have not done as I climbed the corporate ladder. Because of the hurdles I've overcome and the lessons I've learned, I decided to write this book to help women everywhere climb the corporate ladder or to help them understand better how to achieve more within their own businesses.

Nothing in the restaurant industry is easy, so it still bothers me that most people think they can run a restaurant or a restaurant company. The "anyone can flip a burger" mentality and the whole thought process behind it are so wrong. There is so much to running a restaurant. Let me restate that—there is so much to running a successful restaurant operation. I often say with the restaurant business that you either "love it" or you "hate it," and if you love it as I do, you're usually pretty good at it. I get up every day and say, "I *get* to go to work today," not "I *have* to." It's always "I *get* to." I get to make a difference every day—to help all the people who work at our company to grow and develop their skills to be the best they can be—and that is awesome for me.

Since I started at the bottom and worked my way up, I feel that I have a lot to share with other women. Unfortunately, I don't believe women have been the best at mentoring other women or at networking, so I want this book to help fill that gap, and I hope it will serve as a mentor to women, as well as to open their eyes and be a wakeup call to them to help others along the way. If after reading this book, you still have questions or concerns to discuss, I will also make my consulting and speaking talents available to you. I am a firm believer that what goes around comes around—we should treat people like we want to be treated, and we should help anyone and everyone along the way. So writing this book is my way to reach out to many women by offering insights into the corporate world and also insights that will help you, as a woman, to help yourself.

Part 1

FINDING A CAREER

Lesson #1

INTERVIEWING

"Keep true, never be ashamed of doing right; decide on what you think is right and stick to it."
— George Eliot

"I've come to believe each of us has a personal calling that's as unique as a fingerprint—and that the best way to succeed is to discover what you love and then find a way to offer it to others in the form of service, working hard, and also allowing the energy of the universe to lead you."
— Oprah Winfrey

TIPS FOR BEING INTERVIEWED

Let me start by saying that a while back I found myself unemployed for the first time in my life. The following is an article I wrote during that time about women and how they interview:

Women Interview Like They Date

I have come to the conclusion that women job interview like they date—one at a time! This, I have found, is not the way to do it. I can talk about this subject because I have been unemployed for the past fourteen months, and this is the *first* time in my life I've ever been unemployed. I know. I know. I'm not the only one singing this song right now, but let me tell you, it has been an eye-opener for me. For as long as I can remember, if you wanted to work, you could find a job!

Now, I would have to guess that everyone reading this article has either been unemployed herself in the past two years or knows someone who has. I have kept a journal on this journey of the highs, the lows, and the even lower days I've had during the past fourteen months. I decided this week that I would write an article about interviewing, and I hope it will help many of you who are in the middle of this situation or just beginning the process of unemployment.

I began my career in the restaurant business when I was thirteen and my mom bought a small drive-up restaurant. I started working for a big-name fast food company at fifteen, and it's been a restaurant career for me ever since. I continued to grow, develop, and climb the ladder. My last position was president of a restaurant company where we owned and operated seventy restaurants. I have not had to interview for a job in the past twenty-five years, so when I became unemployed in 2009, it was a big learning experience. I want to share what I now know with you. I want you to learn and know how to interview today so you can get that job you want in less time and get back to work.

Men interview like they date: many at the same time! They will interview with any and all headhunters for all job possibilities as much and as often as possible.

Woman interview like they date: they will find one headhunter and wait until he finds them a job interview. Once you start that interview process, you wait and wait until the company wants a second interview with you or your headhunter calls you and says the company has chosen someone else. Then you start the process all over again! Isn't that the way we date? We meet someone. Oh, I like him! He's handsome, nice, and all the other things we say when we meet someone we are interested in. He calls and we start what we believe is our new relationship. We hope each day he'll call, and while we wait, we don't go out looking for anyone else. We wait. We'll go out with our girlfriends, but not to find another guy to date, just to have fun and tell them all about our "new" guy. We are excited, and full of new energy, a new glow. This could be the one!

Then time goes by. You've been on a couple of dates. Things are going well (or so you think), but the next thing you know, it's been a whole week and he has not called you once! Fast forward. It's been three weeks since you've heard from him and now you realize he is *not* interested! There's more drama in those three weeks, but I won't bore you with it because when it's not happening to you, you see it for what it is—then, all you want to do with your girlfriend is shake her and say, "Get over it!" But we don't say anything to our girlfriend because we don't want her doing that to us.

So now the process starts again. We're one or two months older and we're on the manhunt again. Just like job hunting! We're one or two months more broke, besides being older. With the job issue, it's about the money, so we're starting the interviews all over again.

Stop it! We *must* learn how to interview! You must have many, many, I mean fifteen or twenty, headhunters. Each headhunter only gets a few jobs that fit your experience, so if you have fifteen headhunters and each one has a few jobs that would fit your experience, you can find out about forty-five jobs instead of three. Each headhunter with whom you become acquainted will be looking for a job to come across his desk that fits your needs and skills. Now you have a chance of finding that great job in the middle of this double digit unemployment. And once you start interviewing with one company, you *must not* stop communicating with the other fourteen headhunters. You must also go online to look for jobs. There isn't any *one* way to job hunt. Try every way! Headhunters, online sites, networking, job fairs if they have them for your industry, and friends. Do it all! Do it every day! When I decided to get busy and get myself a new position, I told all my friends, "I have a job. My job is to find myself a new great position." I worked every day just like I was going to the office; the only thing is I didn't have to dress up to go to my home office. I did receive unemployment, but as we all know, that is a very small paycheck, but I had a job, the job of looking for a job, and I was bringing in money. Now if I didn't want that small paycheck to continue, I knew what I had to do—get another job!

Too many of the women I talk to now will say, "I received a call from XYZ Company and I'm so excited! It's really the job I want." I reply, "Great! I hope you get that one, but until that company makes you an offer, what have you done today to get a job?" They look at me like I have three heads. Again, they are communicating with *one* company so they don't continue to look for anything else. They almost feel like they'd be cheating on that company, or are not being honest and faithful to a company that *may* or *may not* want to hire them. Please, ladies! We have to get out of our comfort zones and start approaching this process to get the end results we want, a new job as soon as possible!

Interviews all start with phone interviews. You will go through one to four phone interviews before you get to see someone face-to-face. So let's talk about how to project your personality and professionalism through the phone. For those of us who have asked, "Would you like fries with that?" (stop laughing), we have already been through the training classes of smiling with your voice. Employers have many, many people to choose from now so you *must* stand out. They want to hear fun, friendly, passionate, but at the same time, professional and intelligent, not someone who comes across as silly or immature. All they see is your resume and all they hear is your voice. You have to be the person who, when they hang up, makes them think, "I'd really like to talk with her again," or "She's one we can't let get away." You cannot sound desperate, even if you feel it! You are interviewing them as well as they are interviewing you. Get on the Internet and look up the company so you have two to three questions you want to ask before the interview. Most people are proud of the company they work for and are more than willing to share all about the company if you just ask them. Be prepared. Be confident and show them *you* are the best person for the job!

THE VALUE OF BEING A GOOD INTERVIEWER

Now that we've discussed interviewing from the point of how you should approach it, let's discuss interviewing as it pertains to all of you who are doing the hiring and building of great teams. I say often, "We sell pizza, tacos (fill in the blank) to pay the bills, but I am in the *people* business." I believe that with all my heart. It is all about getting all the people in your company who report to you to do what you want, when you want it, how you want it, and with the same passion as you. Wow! That is tiring just to think about, right? Being a great interviewer takes skills, and you need to develop those skills early on in your career.

A lot of managers see interviewing as a chore, but it's really a skill and a vital one if you want a successful team. Sometimes, I hear people say, "I don't need to know all that stuff about interviewing; it's up to HR to do that." Newsflash—not all companies have an HR department, and even companies that do have an HR department may only have one or two people in that department, so you're going to have to help them at some point. And do you want to rely on someone in HR to hire someone who is going to work for you? Wouldn't you rather hire the person *you* think is right for the job? You've heard the saying, "Practice makes perfect." Well, it is so true when it comes to interviewing. Your team reflects you; your team will either make or break you, so if your team is that important, don't you think you should spend a lot of time making sure you get the right team? I do.

Be the best at interviewing. All leaders have people reporting to them. I have found that hiring the right person for the job takes a lot of time and skill; it is one of the most important skills you can learn. Listen to what the interviewee says; do not put words in her mouth. Also, look carefully at a person's work history; remember that past actions will more than likely be future actions. Many people will say only what they think you want to hear when they interview; they have interviewed so much that they just plug in the "right" answers; they say anything to get the job they want. Once you have the person in the company, however, the "real" person comes out and then you have a bigger problem on your hands that is more costly to deal with at that point.

So, one of your biggest assets as an employee and leader is to be a great interviewer. Hire the right person the first time and make sure that person gets the best training. No matter what my position or what my schedule, I make time to have an interview with anyone whom my team wants to hire for a management position. Including myself in the interview process really keeps my managers on their toes; they do not want to send me someone who is not going to be a good addition to our company; it prevents them from doing the "mirror test"—you know what I mean; hold a mirror up to a person's nose and if he fogs it up—meaning he is breathing—hire him.

Another great way to get and keep a good management team is to promote from within, but even that includes interviewing. I love promoting from within; I am so grateful that someone took a chance on me when I did not have the experience or skills. When you promote from within, so many good things are already there; the person already knows the company, you know what kind of worker he is, he knows the company's vision and wants to be part of it, and he is so thankful someone believed in him that he will do all he can not to disappoint you. Companies are always looking for the next great superstar to walk in the door, but seldom do they realize that the best superstar may already be in the company waiting for someone to notice him or her.

David Novak, CEO of Yum Brands, recently wrote the book *Taking People With You* about the concept of promoting from within. This concept is not just for executives but everyone, including entry level managers and their employees who want to be the next shift supervisors. I used to tell my managers that if you spent eight hours in your store today, but you did not teach or develop one person's skills, you did not do your job. Being a successful leader is all about surrounding yourself with successful people and/or surrounding yourself with people who *want* to be successful, and then doing all you can every day to help them achieve their goals. Do not worry about your success; if you do all you can for everyone around you—train, develop, give them the tools, and hold them accountable—you will be more successful than you ever dreamed. They will lift you up—it's called Servant Leadership; I recommend you try it—it works.

Whether you are hiring from within or outside the company, you will need to interview people for various positions. If you have not attended all the "Interviewing 101" classes, I highly recommend you do that. Interviewing is an ongoing skill that you need to set at the top of your list, so any and all classes, seminars, or coaching sessions you can attend—be sure you do. You must learn the legal aspects of hiring; most training classes will give you a one-page handout on the "Do's and Don'ts of Interviewing." Also, take it very seriously when you are learning the "Why's." You will need to teach others how to interview throughout your career, so you need to be able to answer all the questions you will be asked.

In the restaurant business when hiring at the entry level, I stick with the motto "I hire the attitude and train the skill." Do you know what that means? You can hire someone with twenty years experience, who has all the knowledge (or so he thinks) about the job, but if his attitude is bad, he will *not* do a good job for you. I want someone who is really excited about the job, and yes, I know some people cannot get excited about an entry level job, but there are a lot of people who can, and those people are the ones I want.

When you are interviewing entry level people, you are going to want to know what experience they have. Many of them have never worked before so how are you going to find out if they can learn the skills to do the job you have open? First, you have to be able to articulate what job opening you have and exactly what will be that person's job duties. If you don't know what the job is, how will you know if someone can do it? If your company does not have a job description for each position, sit down with the current management team and make one. Once you have determined the job duties, you need to know what hours you have for the job, when the new person should start, who will be training the person, what the pay will be, and all the questions you will want to ask the person during the first interview. Lastly, decide whether you will hire on the first interview or you will have that person return for a second interview.

In almost all interviewing classes, you will learn what the "five-minute interview" is. This interview happens when someone comes in to give you his/her application; right then, you want to take five minutes and find out the basics about this person, including whether they dressed professionally; doing this will help you to avoid wasting his time and yours if you find out in the first five minutes that this job is not a fit.

Create an interviewing schedule and stick with it. For example, you interview every Tuesday and Thursday 2:00 p.m. to 5:00 p.m.—no exceptions. Make sure all employees and managers know it because it will result in a few benefits: 1) it reminds all of your employees that you are always looking for great employees, 2) it will keep them on their toes with their job because they know they can be replaced, and 3) other employees can set up an interview for you without having to ask you or wait until you come in; if someone does a five-minute interview and thinks the interviewee was interesting enough to get a second interview, he can tell the person, "Our manager interviews every Tuesday and Thursday between 2 and 5 p.m. What time can you be here?" It shows your store is organized and ready at all times for interviews and shows how important they are to you as the manager.

When considering whether to have second or third interviews, remember that most potential employees will come in looking really sharp the *first* time, but it's the second and third time they come that they will show their *real* colors. So it's important for you to ask them to come back for another interview. Someone who looks really good on day one could show up completely different the next time.

Before the interview begins, have a notebook and a pen along with your "Ask and Don't Ask" questions. (These should be typed, laminated, and on a clipboard for all to use who are conducting the interview). Once you introduce yourself and shake hands with the interviewee, always say, "I take notes while interviewing to ensure I don't miss anything; is that okay with you?" The purpose here is to let the person know why you are taking notes and to put him at ease. Making the interviewee comfortable is very important; I find that once a person is comfortable with you, he will really open up and talk about who he is, and that's exactly what you want.

Even if you are hiring someone at a higher level, such as a manager, district manager, director of operations, or even higher like a vice president, while it may involve a different conversation, the main point is to remember that all interviewing is still about finding the best person for the job by looking at the person's skills, prior performance, and personality. When you are really good at hiring, you can save the company a lot of money and that makes you a value to that company. Make sure you and your team can hire, train, and develop all the people around you at every level and you will have the best team ever. As I'm known for saying, "Don't worry about yourself; if you take care of all the people who work for you and above you, *they* will take care of you."

Finally, remember that no one ever hires all the right people all the time, but if you really develop your interviewing skills and become really good at it, you will hire the best people, and when you surround yourself with the best people, life feels really good, and it just gets better and better, and who doesn't want that?

Lesson #2

NETWORKING

"Success is not final, failure is not fatal: It is the courage to continue that counts."
— Winston Churchill

Although I feel like all of the information I have written in this book is important, this chapter is one of the most important. I feel most women do not network well. We get so busy with everything that we have to do at work and at home that we don't think about networking, really networking, until we don't have a job, and that is not the time to start.

Truthfully, I never thought much about networking until a few years ago. Oh, I had a lot of women business friends/associates I talked to, but the ones I really had relationships with were the ones working at my current job. Because there were several women I had hired at my previous company, I also stayed in touch with them. Then when I lost my job in 2009, my other women friends and I were all so shocked that it took all of us some time to get our thoughts together to start networking to get me another job. Although I was not the first and would not be the last person to experience a layoff due to the recession, I needed to get a plan together to make sure I would not stay unemployed for long.

I took the first three months just trying to analyze what had happened and getting some long overdue rest. During this time, I realized I had not done a good job of networking. I had been the president of a company, so I had a lot of contacts, and I had a good reputation in the restaurant industry, so now I just needed to reach out and ask people for help. That was the hardest part of all—*asking*. It was not something I'd ever had to do before. Now, here I was without a job, and because the recession was in full bloom, a lot of people needed a job, so I was one of many! Who did I know? What did I want to do? How was I going to do it? Being a successful businesswoman, I knew what had to be done, and I had many successful women friends who could help if I would just reach out and ask.

Once I did ask for help, I found out right away that it was a new day—no longer did wanting a job mean you could have one. Now many companies were doing a lot more with a lot fewer employees, so no matter how many women I knew, at that point, no one had a job for me. My job became finding myself a job.

I had often thought of how it would be to have a job where I could work four days a week, with three days off each week (something that had never been an option when I was in operations). So, I thought, "Well, now's the time. I am going to work Monday through Thursday, 9:00 a.m. to 3:00 p.m. to find another job."

During that time, I needed to reach out to anyone I knew and to others I didn't know to get my name and resume out there. My friends invited me to any networking events they knew of or attended. They also invited me to meet women and men they knew or had met through work or at conventions they had attended; we'd meet for coffee, lunch, or a drink after work.

This process was very hard at first. I was embarrassed to tell people I did not have a job. But I had to get over that embarrassment because it would not pay the bills. So I swallowed my pride and got busy.

I met many headhunters, which is a good way to get and keep your name out there. No matter what job you have, always keep in touch with and reach out to headhunters—that way when they hear of job openings or get the assignment to find a company new employees, your name stays in the top of their minds. I had always been able to meet and exceed my job goals, so now I made my goal not only to get myself a job, but to find a wonderful job, and I knew I could do it. Eventually, a business associate introduced me to a company who was looking for a COO. After about three months of interviewing each other, this company made me an offer I couldn't refuse. Goal accomplished!

I know that between work and family, and trying to have any type of a social life, that adding networking to your "To Do" list seems too hard to find the time for and that you probably feel too tired to make the extra effort. I understand that, but what I really understand is the importance of doing it, so no matter what, you need to schedule time every week that's only devoted to networking. Most of us will do it if we schedule it, so get it on your calendar. Schedule two hours a week at least to meet, call, email, or attend a networking event. Go online and see the companies that are hiring. Read magazines or articles that pertain to your industry so you can keep up on the companies that are doing well, growing, and developing. See who their employees/executives are and make sure you meet them.

It has become the "Who do you know?" game just to get an interview now. Sending your resume online only gets it put in the BIG pile with the hundreds of other resumes, so obviously, that's rarely going to work. However, if you see a job you are really interested in and you cannot find anyone at the company whom you or anyone else knows, you may just have to send in your resume. In that case, you need your resume to stand out. To accomplish that, read up on the company, and use the same verbiage it uses in the ad because the company's sorting system will flag resumes with those words; this method will at least get your resume in the next pile, which could bring it down to being 1 of 100 instead of 1 of 500.

When job hunting, do not get discouraged if you do not hear from the companies where you apply or any of the headhunters right away. A woman who had worked for me in Southern California contacted me to discuss a new job opportunity she had heard about. It was for a franchise that owned and operated about fifty stores and was looking for an employee; she was interested in the job listed. She was excited because it sounded like what she'd been looking for and it was in an area close to where she lived. The company called her and conducted a phone interview, and she was told someone would get back to her by the end of the week. Well, as you can guess, no one had contacted her by Friday, so she called me; my reply was, "Don't worry; just because they said they will contact you by Friday does not mean it will happen, and it does not mean they are not interested. If you really want the job and you have not heard from them by Tuesday, I'd call or email them to express your continued interest." By Tuesday, she still had not heard anything, so she called and got a voicemail box, so she left a professional message, stating that she was interested in the job and was hoping it was still available. When she again didn't hear anything by that next Friday, she called me again. Once again, I told her not to worry, and that just because they had not called did not mean they were not interested. Then she contacted someone she knew who worked there who told her the position had not been filled yet. Five weeks later, the company contacted her; they didn't apologize for keeping her waiting, but they did say they had so many applicants and had been so busy they were just now getting back to those they were really interested in. To make a long story short, she was offered the job, but from first contact to job offer, it took twelve weeks. So do not get discouraged; don't read anything into silence, and don't give up until you've been told the job has been filled—don't stop looking, don't stop interviewing for other jobs, and don't get discouraged—all of this is now part of the *new* job hunting process.

Networking is very important, whether you're looking for a new job or not; you never know what will open up. Don't get so comfortable with your job that you don't continuously see what other opportunities are out there. Also, as you continue to network, you will meet other women looking for jobs, so help them whenever you can. There may not be a job in your company, but you may know someone who knows someone who is looking to fill a position; by forwarding someone's resume with an introduction, you would really be helping someone get a job. I firmly believe that "What goes around comes around." It is always good to help anyone you can; if you've ever been unemployed and not by choice, you know how much you appreciate anything anyone will do to help you. Pay it forward.

Lesson #3

CREATE YOUR DREAM JOB

"People are just as happy as they make up their minds to be."
— Abraham Lincoln

"The only way to do great work is to love the work you do."
— Steve Jobs

Get *or* create the job you've always dreamed about. How? Through direct selling.

Now, before you stop reading because you are thinking you are not a salesperson so this chapter is not for you, let's redefine what a salesperson is and what it means to sell. We all have images of the pushy, irritating salesperson who has given sales a bad name. But sales does not have to be that way. We may not all feel comfortable trying to sell something to people, *but* we all can *tell* everyone about something we believe in; when we talk about something we love or believe in, our passion and belief take over, and before we know it, the person listening is convinced and wants to try the great product we love.

This chapter focuses on the "Tell, Don't Sell" method of making sales, and we can *all* do it. As you can see, it's for anyone who wants a better future—this method allows you the opportunity to create your own job and take control of your future, and nothing makes us feel better than when we feel empowered because we believe in our plan and are able to work at it to bring about results.

Now, before we go further, I don't want anyone to read this chapter and immediately quit her day job. Working in direct sales is a job that takes time because you have to build up clients and sales. It takes time to earn a good income, so you have to keep doing what you are doing while you do direct selling on the side. Now you're thinking, "I don't have time; I'm exhausted now by all that I have to do." I admit direct selling is not for everyone, but for those who choose it, the opportunities and benefits outweigh the obstacles. So as you consider the possibility of direct selling, ask yourself, "Where do I want to be in five years?" Does being your own boss, setting your own hours, and earning a lot of money sound awesome to you? Then let me be the first to say, "One step at a time, one day at a time, and you can/will achieve your goals."

Let me share with you some benefits of having a direct selling business:

1. You will lessen your tax burden because you can write off some of your mortgage since your office will be in your house, and as a result, you'll also be able to write off some of your utility bills. You'll want to check with

your tax accounting expert for more details on these items.

2. You'll be able to work a flexible schedule and set your own hours.
3. You will be your own boss.
4. The more you work and the harder you work, the more money you can make. Your income is not limited by an hourly wage or yearly salary, but limitless.

So how do you begin your direct selling career? First, you have to discover what your passion is. For example, do you like makeup? Then how about selling Mary Kay cosmetics. Do you like to cook? Then try selling Pampered Chef products. There are so many opportunities to choose from. Just get on the computer and look at all the different companies to see which one reaches out and grabs you. Remember, direct selling is not an overnight success idea or a magic wand; this business will take you three to five years to build, but it will be worth it, and don't forget that life is a journey, so have fun along the way.

Not convinced yet? Did you know that approximately twelve million people in the United States are involved in direct selling organizations and another sixty million people worldwide. And guess what? Seventy percent of them are women. What are you waiting for? Financially, you can make a very good living through direct selling, and you can set your own hours, which works well for women with young children who need to work around their schedules. Later in this book are my interviews with successful women, several of whom work in the direct selling industry, so be sure to read their thoughts on why they went into this field and how they feel about that decision.

I chose the corporate life for myself, but it's not for everyone. I love that today we women have so many opportunities and ways to be successful. This world would be so boring if everyone were the same, so thank goodness we are not. Whatever path you choose, be all that you can be, and enjoy the journey.

Lesson #4

EDUCATION

"God will never give us more than we can handle. I just wish He didn't trust us so much."
— Mother Teresa

Education includes both having a college degree and on-the-job experience. Yes, it is important to get a college degree; most executive jobs require it, but I will say not all. Many people simply cannot afford to go to college, but I believe where there's a will, there's a way. You may have to apply for a scholarship or take out a student loan, but in the long run, it will be worth it.

If you need to, there is nothing wrong with working while you go to college; then, by the time you've completed your degree, you not only have a degree but you also have several years of experience too. I call that result a win-win. And employers will take notice that you had the work ethic to do both, as well as that you have some on-the-job experience.

There are so many online schools now that have opened up a lot more opportunities so people can work and go to school at the same time. I believe there is also a "School of Hard

Knocks." In case you've never heard that saying, let me explain it to you. It means learning things the hard way—trial and error—and believe me when I say that some people learn better that way.

While you are working, you can find out if the field you think you want to be in is actually the field you will love once you start working in it. How many times have we heard someone say, "I really thought I wanted to work with the public (or teach, be in sales, etc.), but once I did it, I found out right away that it wasn't for me." So working does many things: it teaches us what we *don't* want to do, what we *do* enjoy doing, and it gives us an income while we are going to school.

Some companies will even pay a percentage of or a set dollar amount toward your education, provided you get a degree you can use to benefit the company for which you are working. Believe me; I know what it feels like to be working and going to school at the same time. It is not easy, but no one said it would be easy; what I will say is, "It's worth it!"

When my son turned sixteen, all he wanted to do was drive just like all other teenagers who want their freedom. I told him he could drive, but he had to pay for his gas because I wanted to make him responsible. Since he was in high school, I agreed he could work on weekends during the school year and anytime in the summer; of course, he needed to stay focused on his grades and school activities.

I remember like it was yesterday when he said to me, "I do not want to work in a restaurant." My first thought was, "Since I've worked in the restaurant business my son's whole life, I must not make it look like much fun!" I told him, "Okay, but at sixteen, I'm not sure where else you will be able to find a job, but go ahead; see what you can find, and bottom line, if you don't work, you don't drive."

I knew how badly he wanted his independence when about two weeks later, he said to me, "Mom, can you help me get a job in a restaurant? I can't find a job anywhere." I did get him an interview, and yes, he did get the job, and it was not long before he told me, "Restaurant work is *not* for me; I hate it." So, see—everyone learns right away that he either loves it or hates it. It's all a part of life's lessons.

Let me add that my son did work at the restaurant for one year before he found himself a job at a music store; no surprise there since he is a drummer, and we both knew that job would be a better fit for him. I am happy to say I did not do a thing to help him with the music store job; he did it on his own. Our children are really much more resourceful than we think they are. I will also brag that he did not just quit his restaurant job; he gave a two weeks' notice and left on good terms. Yes, Mom was proud.

Lesson #5

WORK SMART AND HARD

"I do not know anyone who has gotten to the top without hard work. That is the recipe. It will not always get you to the top, but it will get you pretty near."
— Margaret Thatcher

One of the famous sayings we've all heard many times—heck, we've probably even said it—is "Work smart, *not* hard." Well, I'm here to tell you that in today's economy, you better work smart *and* hard. With the economic climate the way it is today, most companies do more with less. In the days when everyone was making money, companies would have many people in every department; now, if you want to keep your job, you need to be able to do several things and not complain about it. When companies start downsizing, they still need everything done that they did before, but they have to do it with less people, so they need employees who are willing to say, "Yes, "Yes," and "Yes" to whatever jobs need to be done. If you want to keep or find a job, you better be one of those employees.

This need to work smart *and* hard became a reality for me when the recession was in full swing in 2008-2009 and we had a position that needed filling. When I did an exit interview for the person leaving, I discovered that this employee had really been doing about three jobs; we all knew during this time that everyone's workload had increased because our company had also had to cut back, but that meant that trying to replace this person would be more difficult than usual. We ended up hiring someone to fill the "main" job who also was talented enough to pick up other tasks. And then we spread out the rest of the work to the other employees. In this economic climate, people are so thankful to have their jobs that they are willing to do more to keep them; to keep the company financially stable, everyone did everything that he or she could.

So now we are working smarter *and* harder—I think that needs to be our new slogan.

But while we all may be working harder, let me add here something from my heart: Don't be so busy "climbing the ladder," getting the next promotion or the next raise that you don't enjoy life. There will always be the next something to achieve, but I'm sure we've all heard the saying that no one on his deathbed has ever said that he wished he had worked more. How true that is. Just stop a minute and think when you are on your deathbed, "What will I wish I had done more of?" Then make sure you do it. No regrets! Life is too short. Being the next supervisor, director, vice president, president, CEO, or COO is nice—it's even good in many ways, including financially. But more than anything, being happy and being proud of who you are is really the best position to be in.

Part 2

BEING A COMPANY ASSET

Lesson #6

DON'T LET PEOPLE DISMISS YOU BECAUSE YOU'RE A WOMAN

"The whole point of being alive is to evolve into the complete person you were intended to be."
— Oprah Winfrey

We've all heard that it's a man's world, and as a result, it's tempting to think we have to act like men and play by their rules, but the only way we can change that is to refuse to do so. Stay feminine; do not try to dress or act like a man. Don't cuss, tell raunchy jokes, or participate in male bantering. Be proud to be a woman—you can be strong, intelligent, funny, and very successful just being who you are. The only male trait you need to copy is not to be emotional; deal with facts not feelings. That's just life in the corporate world.

I *love* being a woman; I wouldn't change it for anything. I am still surprised that well into the twenty-first century, women still feel like they have to fit into a man's world to get ahead in the workplace and that some men still prefer to work with just men rather than women. This kind of sexism, intentional or not, is still an issue, even though many successful women in the past twenty years have really opened doors for women everywhere. Don't be fooled that this issue no longer exists because it does. Let me give you a personal example of something that happened to me.

I was president of a company that at the time employed over 2,000 people in two different states. The vice president of operations (a man) and I were at a large franchise convention. There were lots of vendors with booths to display their products or services in hopes of obtaining more business. As the vice president and I were walking around the vendor booths, making new contacts, reconnecting with our current vendors, and really enjoying ourselves, we stopped at a booth that had several male salespeople. We struck up a conversation with them about their products and services. Then one sales guy pulled out his business card, turned to the vice president of our company, handed him his card, and said, "I'd like to do business with your company; call me when you get back and we'll schedule time to get together."

What was especially discouraging about this situation was that we both had introduced ourselves and this guy had asked what we did at the company, so he already knew I was the president and would be the ultimate decision-maker. But I guess this salesperson didn't hear, or he just didn't feel comfortable dealing with a woman. Let me add that my vice president instantly said, "If you want to work with us, then you will need to meet with her since she's the president of our company." We both just smiled and shook hands with everyone and walked to the next booth. Later, my vice president said, "I guess he doesn't want to deal with women." I laughed and said, "Well, he won't get much business if he doesn't."

So see, sexism is still an issue but not one that can't be overcome with grace, professionalism, and focusing on working with people who do feel women can run companies and can do a great job at every level.

Lesson #7

DON'T BE EVERYTHING TO EVERYONE

"You know, if you just set out to be liked, you would be prepared to compromise on anything, wouldn't you, at any time? And you would achieve nothing!"
— Margaret Thatcher

Don't try to be everything to everyone. Because nurturing is in a woman's nature, I have seen too many women fall all over themselves trying too hard. Do not jump up and make coffee if that's not in your job description. Do not wait on any man just because you are the female in the room. Men are capable of getting whatever they need whenever they need it, and they will look at you differently when you wait on them.

Once when I was attending a monthly executive meeting, we discussed what things needed to happen at the upcoming franchise meeting. Some of us would be presenting at the franchise meeting, and others would be there just to be available before and after to help any franchisee that needed it. We were discussing which department/person in our meeting would be responsible for each item needed for the meeting. One of the items was breakfast pastries and coffee. Since I was the only woman in that meeting, I was *sure* they would all look at me and say, "Nina, why don't you take care of that." I thought this not because I had ever done it for them before but just because I was the only female in the room. I was a director at that time, and everyone else in the room was also a director who headed a different department, except for the president, who was also in the room; we all reported to him.

Much to my surprise, when the president came to the breakfast items, he went right to one of the guys who was not making a presentation at the meeting. Of course, the other guys started to laugh, and after everyone looked around, especially at me, the person chosen said, "Okay, no problem; just one thing—I don't know how to make coffee." At first, everyone was quiet. Then the president started to laugh and said, "Well, you have three weeks to learn." We all chuckled and went on with the rest of the meeting.

So *some* men do get it, but you *must* make sure they see you as "very good at your job." You are not looking for special treatment; you just want the same opportunities as the men have. Don't try to be all things for everyone. Just strive to be the best person for the job—not the best *man* (or woman) for the job.

Lesson #8

TRAIN YOUR BRAIN

"It is not the strongest of the species that survive, nor the most intelligent, but the one most responsive to change."
— Charles Darwin

"Forty-five seconds or less." Learn how to say everything you want to say in forty-five seconds or less. To do this, you must know the topic you want to talk about. Like most of my life and career lessons, I learned this lesson the hard way. Let me tell you the story.

When I worked in the Training Department, I reported to the VP of Training and Development. One day when I went to his office and told him, "I have a situation I want to discuss with you." Before I could sit down or even start with my story, he stopped me and said, "Whatever you have to say, I want you to say it in forty-five seconds or less." He was serious. I was shocked because he had never talked to me like that before, and I was not sure exactly why he was now. I stopped and looked at him (doing the best I could to have no expression). I wanted to think carefully before I said anything. He then said, "I recently read this book *Everything*

You Need to Say in 45 Seconds or Less." (Well, that answered my question of why he said that to me.) He continued, "So, I've decided to be more efficient with our time. I am going to require this team to read this book and to follow it." I was still standing between the door and the seats in front of his desk. He then said, "Tell me in forty-five seconds the bottom line to your story, and if I need any more information, I'll ask for it." Well, as you can imagine, I thought, "How rude! I have a whole story to tell you so you will really know what happened, but you don't want to hear it."

Of course, I didn't say that; I thought for another minute and gave him the forty-five-second version. He had a couple of questions, but I did not elaborate; I just answered what he asked; he then gave me his recommendation, and without further ado, I went back to my desk.

I must have had the "I can't believe that just happened" look on my face because one of the guys in our department looked at me and asked, "What's wrong?" I just shook my head and said, "Nothing." I really needed to digest what had happened to figure out how I felt about it before saying anything.

About thirty minutes later, the VP came into our area and gave each of us the book. He went through the same speech he had given me and that was that. It took a while, but I really did come to understand the meaning of that book. The point isn't that everything has to be said in forty-five seconds, but that a lot of time is spent on unnecessary details and explaining how we feel about something, which isn't really relevant to the facts. Years ago, there was a TV series in which one of the characters had a familiar line, "Just the facts, ma'am." I don't say "ma'am," but I often do say "Just the facts!"

Today, I try to teach this lesson to others. Wasting time is unacceptable, especially in this day and age where so many things are vying for every minute we have. I would never want anyone to think I don't value his or her opinions, but in business, we are doing people a favor when we teach them to focus on facts and to get to the point quickly so we can save time and define the real issue. Save the feelings conversations for girlfriend time.

Lesson #9

FIND A MENTOR—BE A MENTOR

"You get in life what you have the courage to ask for."
— Oprah Winfrey

Find a mentor—be a mentor. Many women would be willing to help other women with their careers, but until someone asks them, they don't put much thought into it. In our busy, fast paced life not many people make time to mentor. If you're lucky, someone will mentor you, but don't wait for it to happen. Don't be afraid to find a mentor for yourself.

Never be afraid to ask someone to share her knowledge and talents with you; people will feel honored that you asked them. Men learn to seek out mentors at a young age and think nothing about it; they almost expect the senior executives to bring them along and set them up for success. When was the last time you saw or heard of a woman doing that?

I have a dear friend who opened my eyes to this situation a few years ago. We met through a work association. One day, I asked her about her career plans. "What do you want to do, and is it with your current company, or is there a company out there you'd really like to work for?" She didn't really have an answer; she wasn't sure, but one thing she was sure about was that there were no female executives in her company who worked in her department or even in close proximity to her from whom she could learn. "That's not good," I replied.

We continued to talk for a bit, and I was trying to think whether I knew anyone or I could help her in any way. When I started telling her about the things I teach my team, she perked up and said, "I would really love to learn more about your profit and loss statements; it would help me in my business, and I would feel much better being able to have a conversation on that topic if I really understood the business aspects of all those numbers; would you teach me?" "Yes, absolutely I'll teach you," I told her. "We'll have a business meeting once a month. I'll give you homework, and you can learn on your time how and where the numbers come from for an understanding of how you can help effect them in a positive way to help people make more money." She was so excited then, and I was thrilled that I could help her.

What we need to realize is that most women are afraid to ask for help or advice; they do not want anyone to know they don't know that (whatever "that" is). And then when they figure out they need to know it, they don't know who will help them instead of judging them. Be the woman who "pays it forward." Be the women who reaches out and helps without being asked and who makes time to help others when asked.

Whatever it is that you are good at, set up a training class for that skill or topic without being asked. Post on the employee board, or wherever it will be seen, a notice that says something like:

I will be conducting an Interviewing Class

Tuesday from 2:00 to 4:00 p.m.

at the ABC store

Anyone and everyone is invited!

You will be surprised by who will show up. And if no one shows up, that's okay. Do it again the next week. If no one shows up again, bring work you can do for those two hours (you can still be productive). You are still showing everyone that interviewing is your strength, you are willing to help anyone, and you are willing to share your knowledge to make the company better. Trust me; it won't go unnoticed.

Now, for those women who have a VP position or above, being a mentor is a responsibility we should never take lightly. Give back and support any organization that helps women in whatever capacity you choose. I believe we typically choose to help where we've been hurt. If we come from a household of abuse and we overcome that life, then when we can, we'll go and volunteer to help women who are abused. Similarly, if you've struggled in your career because it has been male-dominated, then help women who are starting their careers as a great way to give back.

One word of caution: Do not get too attached to your mentor. You cannot forget that work is work. Do not start telling her about your personal business because it may come back to bite you. You want to make sure you learn all you can from your mentor, but you do not need to feel like you are "girlfriends" or best friends because that is not the case. There may be times when you meet your mentor outside the workplace, but that does not mean you are friends. You can be friendly but not friends. Be professional at all times. If you keep the same mentor for years—and I hope you do—you will develop a friendship that may last the rest of your life, but when you start with your mentor, keep it strictly business and keep it professional. She will appreciate that.

We all have something we can share. A saying I've coined is, "Being a good leader means I will share what I know and learn what I don't know." Seek a mentor. Be a mentor. Both are rewarding.

Lesson #10

LEARN THE GOOD, THE BAD, & THE UGLY FROM YOUR BOSS

"When one door closes, another opens; but we often look so long and so regretfully upon the closed door that we do not see the one that opened for us."
— Alexander Graham Bell

Remember, you learn what you want to be *and* what you don't want to be from people you work with and for. I do think we can learn something from all people in business; at times, you may say to yourself, "I never want to be like him/her," but even those people teach you something, and you should always remember their behavior so you do not repeat it. Here are a few examples of people I've learned from.

THE GOOD

My first general manager job was exciting and hard all at the same time. I often say, "I had more energy than brains at that point." My district supervisor was one of the toughest and best bosses I ever had. I thought everyone wanted to be as successful as I did, but I learned the hard way that that was not the case.

I needed another shift manager, so I decided to train one of my employees for the job. We discussed what the job was, and she said she was interested, so I went full speed ahead with her training. After I had spent countless hours with her and she was almost done with the training, she called in sick one day; I thought, "That's odd; she's never sick, but okay."

The next day, she called in sick again; now I really thought something was wrong, and I was right; she came to work the next day and asked whether she could talk to me alone. She said she had changed her mind and didn't want the management job, and she said she had known it a couple of weeks earlier but didn't want to tell me. I have to admit I was surprised and disappointed, in part because I thought she would be good at it, and in part because I had spent so much time and energy on her that I didn't understand why she hadn't told me earlier. I told her, "Okay, you can be just an employee," and we went back to work.

Yes, I agree—I did not handle that well at all. The next day when my boss arrived at my store, I told him what had happened. He sat me down and had a long talk with me. He told me, "Not everyone wants to be successful like you do. We need employees at every level, and the best thing you can do is help them by training and developing them to be the best they can be at whatever positions they want to be in." That was the best thing he could have said to me, and I have lived by it and taught it to all my managers ever since. And yes, that employee stayed my day employee; she did a great job and never went into management.

THE BAD

One of the first managers I worked under was a young lady in her early twenties, and I did not like her management style at all. She yelled at people in front of everyone, and she would grab people by the arm, take them to the place where they were supposed to be, and overall, did her best to humiliate people every day. Of course, my first thought was, "I'm quitting. I don't want to work for someone like that!" But if you know me at all, you know I am not a quitter! So I decided I would learn from her what I never wanted to be and that's what I did. Yes, she was soon terminated (of course, not soon enough for my liking). Meanwhile, I continued working and eventually became the store's general manager.

The lesson here: Never walk off the job! I don't care how "right" you think you are, how upset you are, or how badly someone treated you. You don't have to stay at a job where you are mistreated or unhappy, but you do need to leave the right way. Yes, there is a right way to leave a job. First, find another job—it is always easier to get a job when you have a job. Do not forget that! Then when you do find another one, give an appropriate two weeks' notice at the job you are leaving and leave on good terms. You never know when someone from your former job might resurface in your work life again.

THE UGLY

When I worked as director of operations for a franchisee in Southern California, I learned many priceless things, including how unprofessional and pretty disgusting someone in authority can act because of that power. The previous director of operations had recently left the company and the owner had promoted me to take that position. At this time, we had ten restaurants and we were growing, which was a very exciting time for the company.

We had been contacted by the franchisor about a meeting in San Diego, which was about sixty or so miles from us. I knew this meeting was important for both of us to attend, but at times, the franchisee was known not to attend meetings. This particular time, he said he would go and he wanted us to ride together. Riding together was unusual since we both were very busy and usually would be going in different directions after the meeting, so taking our own cars worked better for us. This time, however, since he wanted to ride together, I agreed.

I met him at the office and we took his car. We drove to the meeting, discussing business issues on the way, so the drive went by fast. After the meeting, it was about 1:00 p.m. so we started back. He said he was hungry and knew of a place about halfway back where we could stop. When we got there, the restaurant was busy and the hostess said the wait would be about thirty minutes, but they did have some tables in the bar area. He said, "We'll sit in the bar." So we did, which was not a big issue for me since I thought we both had things scheduled for the afternoon and I didn't want to wait thirty minutes to be seated. Right away, he ordered a drink—yes an alcoholic drink, which surprised me, not because he didn't drink, but because it was the middle of the day and we still had about a forty-five-minute drive back.

When the waitress came to take our order, I ordered a salad and he said, "I am going to have oysters, yes, raw oysters, and bring me a beer too." Now I was thinking, "This is not good." I was feeling a bit uncomfortable since he drove there and now he was drinking too much to drive back. He then proceeded to down his first drink and start on the beer and the oysters. He continued to eat oysters and discuss why people love oysters, and yes, what he said was inappropriate. He became much more relaxed, more talkative, and a bit on the too friendly side. I finally had to say, "I know you are enjoying yourself, but I need to get back to work."

The waitress came over after his second beer and said, "I sure hope you're not driving." Then she looked at me and he said, "I will let her drive my car." I said, "That's good because I wouldn't ride with you, and I was wondering who I was going to call to come and get me." I said it lightheartedly—he was my boss after all—but I was not planning on getting in the car with him driving.

Yes, I did drive his car back to the office, and believe me, the drive back was uncomfortable. I asked him whether someone would pick him up at the office and he finally agreed he'd call someone and not drive. This situation did not surprise me as he had been a bit too friendly from time to time, although I had made it perfectly clear I was not interested in anything outside of a professional relationship. I did feel he thought his behavior was fine because he is the boss and I worked for him.

We all know someone who has been in this situation; it might even have been you. Just remember that even if someone is the boss, it does not give that person "privileges." You have the right to say, "No." You have the right to tell the person it is not appropriate for him or her to act like that with you.

The next day, he acted like it had never happened, and I didn't mention it either. Nor did I ride with him to any more meetings (I learned that lesson). When we had meetings to go to, I always said, "I need to drive my car because I have an appointment after the meeting." He never said anything other than, "Okay, see you there."

List 5 people you have worked for/with, from whom you have learned positive work skills:

1. ______________________________

2. ______________________________

3. ______________________________

4. ______________________________

5. ______________________________

List 5 people you have worked for/with, who exhibited work skills you never want to emulate:

1. ______________________________

2. ______________________________

3. ______________________________

4. ______________________________

5. ______________________________

Go back now, and beside each person's name, list the behavior he or she displayed.

Of the negative skills listed, are there any you think you might exhibit, and what can you do to change that situation so you are not a bad role model to others?

Of the positive skills listed, how might you exhibit those skills better in the workplace to help others?

Lesson #11

FAKE IT TILL YOU MAKE IT

"When it comes to the future, there are three kinds of people: those who let it happen, those who make it happen, and those who wonder what happened."
— John M Richardson Jr.

Fake it till you make it. In the restaurant business, this saying means: put on that smile, be happy even if you don't feel happy, and if you do it long enough, you will become happy. Do not bring your moods, your temperament, your personal issues, family issues, or anything else in those categories to work.

Men always think women are too emotional, so don't give them any reason to think you fit that stereotype. We women have to be very careful in this area because when we are women and we aren't emotional, men also have a hard time trying to figure that one out. I once had a boss who called me "Hard Hearted Hannah" because I did not get emotional around him; I was all about business and the policies and procedures that needed to be followed, but he wasn't like that. I do, however, think he liked my professionalism because he couldn't be like that and wanted to be. He promoted me three times, which proves I was capable and the best person for the job.

Now, I'm not saying you have to be hardhearted; that doesn't work for anyone; nor do I think I am. Remember, not everything is black and white. What I am saying is to leave your troubles at the door. When you enter work, smile and get to business. When I ask general managers, "What is one quality you like in your employees?" they always reply "No drama." You want to be the employee who does *not* bring drama to the workplace, and just because it's *your* drama does not make it special or okay. All the reality shows on TV today really encourage drama in every episode; it seems people love to watch people act like that, but trust me, don't act that way at work. Managers and employees both have so many things to deal with on a daily basis that employee drama is not welcomed nor accepted for very long, no matter what position you hold.

Here's my question: Which one are you? The drama queen, or the worker bee?

Think about a time when you brought drama to work with you. What happened?

If you could go back and do that day over, what would it look like?

Lesson #12

YOUR OWN SPECIAL STYLE

"Remember always that you have not only the right to be an individual; you have an obligation to be one."
— Eleanor Roosevelt

Remember, everyone brings his or her own special style to a job. Don't try to be anyone else; just be *you*, and the best *you* possible.

Being the best *you* means you feel very comfortable in your own skin, comfortable in your job knowledge, and comfortable with who you are. How many times have you met someone and thought, "She is fake"? Although, that person doesn't think anyone else knows she's a fake because she thinks she's so good at acting that no one can tell. If the fake one is you, please let me tell you that everyone can tell.

When I was a district supervisor, I was transferred to take over a district that had eight stores. After a few weeks of observing the teams and managers in each store, it quickly became apparent that most of the general managers did not have the skills needed to be in the positions they were in, but one especially stood out as lacking in restaurant and management skills—she had been given the general manager position because of whom she knew rather than what she knew. I continued to hear from a couple of executives about how talented she was, but rather than add anything to that conversation, I decided to spend time in her store and give her the benefit of the doubt in hopes that she did have talent and I just wasn't yet able to see it.

I spent the next two months working with this general manager, and it became very clear that she did not have a clue how to run that restaurant. In fact, she had two really good shift supervisors and some good employees at her restaurant who were the ones keeping the restaurant going. She did not understand any of the numbers on her P&L (profit and loss statement), and no one before me ever met with her about her numbers. Because of whom she knew, no one wanted to lose his or her job, so everyone just let her do what she wanted, which did not teach her anything. You do not do people a favor when you do not expect anything from them. As managers and executives, it's our job to teach, coach, and help people develop their skills and then hold them accountable; that is the only way they will grow.

After several weeks of creating documentation for this general manager, I had a meeting with the executives who had put her in this position. In detail, I laid out the store's operation, her lack of skills for this particular position, and then concluded with, "She doesn't know what she doesn't know." After I let that sink in, I added, "I am going to demote her and put her in a position where she can learn from a strong general manager all the skills she needs to be successful. If I keep her in her current position, I will only end up terminating her for lack of performance. Meanwhile, the two shift managers she has—which I might add, she did not hire but inherited—have done a good job of keeping the restaurant running, and with a good general manager, both of them could be promoted to an assistant manager position when one becomes available."

The next day, I scheduled a meeting with this general manager at a different restaurant. I went through with her all the issues at her store, and I discussed with her that she did not know what she did not know. There is so much more to running a successful restaurant than showing up, serving the guests, and closing the store. After a long talk, she began to cry and expressed to me how hard it had been on her; she wanted to do a good job, but she didn't know how, so she had "faked" it every day, and she was exhausted. She knew she needed help, but by this time, she said, "if I had asked for help, then they would know I did not know and I couldn't have that." I gave her a few days off and then she came back to work at a different restaurant as a shift supervisor; she did want to learn more, and the general manager at the new restaurant was someone she felt comfortable with and could learn from.

We ended the situation well, but it was not easy; many people came to me, saying, "If you mess with her, you could lose your job." I realized this, but I could not let someone stay in a position who could not do the job; it wasn't right for her or for her employees, and overall, not right for the company. I couldn't be fake by letting her continue, and she was tired of being fake.

When you spend so much time and energy trying to be someone else, you have to be exhausted. There is only one you, so be you, every day for the rest of your life. Enjoy you, and if there's things about you that you don't like, change them; change can only come from you. Don't hide it; change it.

Lesson #13

LISTEN TO RADIO STATION WIIFM&C

"I don't believe you have to be better than everybody else. I believe you have to be better than you ever thought you could be."
— Ken Venturi

Do not say or agree to a task or job that you do not believe is achievable. Volunteering for a new task to learn something new is not what I mean here. What I am talking about is being pressured into agreeing with something you know is not going to happen.

Here's an example: You are setting your next month's goal and you write down that you can increase sales 10 percent. You must be sure you can do the 10 percent or more before you ever agree to it. If you say 10 percent and you only deliver 5 percent, no matter the reason, your word will be worth a little less in the eyes of your coworkers or employers.

My point is that in business and in life, whether you are male or female, it is important to keep your word—achieving more is good, but achieving less is unacceptable. I have seen a person talk his team members into agreeing with him that they can increase sales more than what that team thought possible. Guess what happened? When they did not achieve that goal, the head of that department threw them under the bus. Is that fair? You're right; it's not, but we don't live in "fair"—we live in reality.

When you don't think that what your boss wants is possible, you are going to have to be a good communicator and be able to tell him why it's not possible, and don't forget to say what is possible. You never want to go to your boss without options, without ways to get to the place he wants to be with clear concise details for how you will make it happen.

Now, with all that said, if there is a job or task that needs to be done and you would like to do it, but you know you need different skills, it is appropriate to say, "I would really like to do that, but at this time, I do not have the skills needed, so I would like to get training, attend classes, whatever is available to learn the skills." Then, it would be very wise to add, "Teaching me would be a cost savings to the company because once I'm trained, I'll be able to save the company money so it won't have to hire someone else to do the job or outsource it." Getting your boss to agree to this kind of proposal is a win-win for you and for the company; you get more skills to add to your resume, and the company will then have someone to do the job needed without adding to its payroll.

There is one radio station all employees listen to: WIIFM (What's In It For Me). Instead of listening to that station, listen to the one that few listen to: WIIFM&C (What's In It For Me *and* the Company). Listening to WIIFM&C will bring success for both the company and its employees. Plus, you will be the "exception." You will stand out, and as a leader, that's exactly what you want to do—Stand Out. So stand up and be noticed for all the qualities and value you bring to the company.

Lesson #14

ALWAYS SHARE YOUR KNOWLEDGE

"If your actions inspire others to dream more, learn more, do more and become more, you are a leader."
— John Quincy Adams

Never be afraid of sharing your knowledge. The more you teach, train, coach, and develop all the people around you, the better the company will become, and you will be a big part of that. A lot of people feel they need "job security." They want to be the only one who has certain knowledge because they are insecure—don't be that person. Be the person who is secure in her leadership role; act like the leader to be seen as the leader. A leader will share all she knows, *and* she will learn what she doesn't know. When the people who work for you develop greater skills and knowledge, they will get you promoted, not fired; being a leader will help you help others, and those others will help you in return; that is what should happen.

Even if you do not want to be promoted, still be a good leader and do all the things I've just said. You should take pride, regardless, in seeing your employees get promoted within your company or seeing them reach out to another company to move up the ladder. It is great to be known in a company as the person who produces great people; many people will then want to work for you because they have seen or have been told of all the people you trained and developed who have been promoted. You will be the "go to" person for career advancement. You will be known as the best person in your field. Wow! What a great place to be.

List people you have shared your knowledge with and the information or skills you taught them:

Now make a list of people with whom you currently work or with whom you know you could share your knowledge. Next to each name, write the information or skill you can teach him or her:

Lesson #15

TO MOVE UP, YOU HAVE TO LOOK UP

"The whole point of being alive is to evolve into the complete person you were intended to be."
— Oprah Winfrey

If you want to move up, you have to look up. Find out what your boss wants and be the first one to do it. Learn how to manage up and manage down.

MANAGE UP

Managing up means making sure you have the same vision and goals as your boss—and then doing everything you can to help achieve them. Most managers spend all their time managing the people who report to them, and they think that's all they are supposed to do; those managers are missing the big picture. When executives are looking inside an organization to see whether there is anyone to promote, you want to be the one they notice. If you look/act too busy or too stressed, it does not make you look good at your job or even competent; it looks like you are dog paddling as fast as you can to stay afloat, and that is not the image they want to represent them. You have to make your job look comfortable for you—enjoyable, very manageable—and you must have great numbers. Also, develop people who can take over your job so you can move up the ladder; otherwise, management might feel it can't replace you in your current position so you will be stuck there. In short, don't get the reputation that you don't work very much or that you work too much.

There may be times when you have a boss who is very insecure; he or she will be uncomfortable with you because you're smart, personable, and good at your job with a desire to have his/her job. What do you do in this situation? This is where really good people skills come in; you want to make your boss successful in a way that is non-threatening to both you and him. Find out what your boss's goals are and then help him to achieve them. I think being a good manager at any level is defined by: helping all others to reach their goals, which will ensure the company or organization reaches and exceeds its goals.

Remember, keep your boundaries; don't mix personal and business. Stay focused on the big picture and be better today than you were yesterday.

Lesson #16

LIFT UP OTHER WOMEN

"What is the recipe for successful achievement? To my mind, there are just four essential ingredients: Choose a career you love…Give it the best there is in you…Seize your opportunities…And be a member of the team."
— Benjamin F. Fairless

Lift up other women. Find the good in them no matter what their positions; women are especially energized by people believing in them. Be that confident, professional woman who does not feel threatened by other women. I am often heard repeating the saying, "What goes around comes around." When we look for the good in others and encourage them to use their gifts to be the best they can be, people do not forget that; remember, people may forget your name, people may forget what you've done, but people will *not* forget how you made them feel.

Help other women feel good about themselves. Look for things about them to compliment, but remember, you must be genuine when you give compliments; people can tell immediately when you're being fake. If you look long enough, you can find the good in people. Look for the skills others have and help them to strengthen those skills and use them to their and the company's benefit.

People, both men and women, also feel good when you ask them to teach you something. Asking to be taught something is a compliment in itself because it shows that you recognize that person's talent, skills, or knowledge. You have to be careful in business, however, with this opportunity to learn; your teacher should be someone at your level or just one level above you. When you need to learn a new skill, you don't go to the top executives to ask; they are very busy, and instead of seeing your request as a compliment, they will think you are a pest and you must really have a lot of nerve to ask them. I'm not saying here that most executives think they're better than everyone else; they are just very busy, so unless they approach you to mentor or teach you, don't bother them; find a peer or your boss to ask for help or mentoring, and keep it that way at every level you climb.

Make sure you never go overboard with the compliments because you could come off as looking like you're kissing up, and you don't want that. Give credit where credit is due; do not take the credit for something you did not do, and if you are getting credit for something your team did, be sure to give the team credit; keep yourself humble and thankful, and surround yourself with awesome people. You want to hire people who are good at the job you want them for. Do not feel intimidated when they have skills that are better or different than yours in certain areas; those people will just make you and your team look really good, so bring in the best and the brightest.

List five women you know and the talents/skills that you are going to praise them for:

1. ______________________________

2. ______________________________

3. ______________________________

4. ______________________________

5. ______________________________

Lesson #17

DETERMINE YOUR STRENGTHS AND YOUR WEAKNESSES

"Everything that happens to you is a reflection of what you believe about yourself. We cannot outperform our level of self-esteem. We cannot draw to ourselves more than we think we are worth."

— Iyanla Vanzant

Realize your strengths *and* your weaknesses. *All* of us have weaknesses—it's how we deal with them that will either make us successful or hold us back. Once you realize your weaknesses, you can hire someone who is strong in the areas where you are weak. You do not have to be—nor are you expected to be—the best at everything. What you are expected to do is to make sure that in the areas where you are responsible for the results, you produce the best results possible. That's what makes a good leader.

When I was a district manager, I had a manager who was excellent at customer service and could build sales like no one else—definitely a strength. However, he did not like paperwork; as a result, he did not keep up with all the paperwork his job mandated he do. I would hear comments from different departments that "The manager of Store X never turns in his paperwork on time," or I would hear people on the phone with this manager, insisting he get some form to them that they were waiting on.

After I had heard about this situation several times, I went to his store and spent some time talking with him. I asked him whether there were any reasons why he was having problems getting his paperwork to the office correctly and on time. He said, "No, I'm just busy, but I'll make sure I get on top of it right away." Of course, I knew if he could do it, he would do it; he was a good employee/manager and not the type to do only what was required of him.

After that, I kept an ear open, but I only heard that the same issues were still happening, so I knew it was time to get him some help. He was struggling with how to do the paperwork, and he was too embarrassed to tell us because he thought not being good at everything made him less than he wanted to be. He thought he would not be able to keep his job because he couldn't do it *all*.

To resolve the situation, I decided we would bring in an assistant manager whose strength was completing paperwork, and I assigned him to this store management's team. Then the store had the best of both—someone who could increase sales, and someone who would make sure all the office paperwork was complete and turned in on time. That solution created a win-win for everyone. We must understand that we don't have to be good at everything, but we do have to recognize what we are not good at and employ someone who is. Recognizing your own weaknesses and finding a way around them—now that's a strength.

We can't, of course, capitalize on our strengths or resolve our weaknesses until we know what they are. So, take some time to determine your strengths and weaknesses. Make your own list, and don't be afraid to ask your coworkers, boss, employees, or other people close to you what they think are your strengths and weaknesses. You may be surprised to find you have strengths you didn't realize, and in time, hopefully you'll appreciate the honesty in learning whether you have weaknesses you didn't know so you can improve them.

Below, list all of your strengths:

Now let's list your weaknesses:

What can you do so you can devote more of your time to using your strengths for your and your company's benefit?

Which of your weaknesses would you like to turn into strengths?

How could you turn those weaknesses into strengths?

For the weaknesses that you don't feel you can turn into strengths, what can you do so they do not hold you back? For example, finding someone else who can help you.

Part 3

WORKPLACE ISSUES *and* HOW TO SOLVE THEM

Lesson #18

WORK IS NOT A DATING SERVICE

"Men always want to be a woman's first love—women like to be a man's last romance."
— Oscar Wilde

Work is not a pick up place or a place you get paid to find a date. Never date, sleep with, hook up with, or get emotionally or physically involved with anyone at work. No matter whether you work for him, he works for you, or he works in another department, it will not work out.

Think about it—what happens when you break up? Oh, so now you're saying, "We won't break up." Okay, let's take a stroll down that lane; say you don't break up and you end up getting married; then what? Do you think you both will be able to keep the same jobs you currently have? Better yet, will you get promoted? This stuff happens all the time and it does not work out for the best. Keep personal matters away from work.

In all the years I've been in the restaurant business, this rule against dating in the workplace has not changed. I was having coffee with the president of another restaurant group in the Northwest when he asked me, "Why do you think workplace dating is so prominent in the restaurant industry?" I replied that I think it's because we are a passionate group of people who spend a lot of time at our jobs and we have a lot in common, so when you think about it, those items are what most relationships are made of. As coworkers, we have a lot to talk about and we understand the issues that we're having, so that brings people together, and when that happens—well, other things happen too.

Again, that is my opinion, but I have seen this situation happen for years, and as I've said, it has not changed.

Here's an example of mixing business with pleasure that ended with someone losing her job: I had a manager who had worked for me for years; she was very good at her job and loved what she did. In our many conversations about her goals and what she aspired to do, she told me she would love to meet someone and some day get married and have a couple of children. She also said she always wanted to keep working, but she was not interested in moving up the corporate ladder. I love it when people are honest with me because my goal is to help them to be the best they can be at whatever it is they want to do, but if they are not honest with what they want to do, then both our time and energy is wasted because we are trying to reach a goal that does not exist.

About a year later, this manager called me and asked whether I would come by her store; she needed to talk to me. During our face-to-face meeting, she told me she was five months pregnant, and she thought she'd better tell me so we could start training someone to take over for her while she was out having the baby. That made sense to me. I congratulated her and we discussed people we had in the restaurant and what needed to happen in the next several months since we only had three months to replace her before she went on maternity leave. She also told me the father would not be involved, so she would be a single mom, but she would be back as soon as she could. She worked up until about three weeks before the baby was due.

Once this manager left on maternity leave, I started hearing things in the restaurant about a relationship between her and one of the kitchen staff. When another manager asked me whether I knew about that situation, I said, "No, she told me the dad was not in the picture." That manager did not say anymore, and although I felt there was more to know about the situation, I decided I'd wait and ask her about it later.

When the baby was born, she texted me, and then she called me a few weeks later so we could meet to discuss her return. I was anxious for her return, but because of the talk going around the restaurant, I knew it was time to have a "heart to heart" with her before she came back. I always believe there is "some" truth to rumors; it may not all be true in the way it's told, but somewhere, something is true, and what better way to get to the truth than by asking? We scheduled a time to meet at the restaurant. She was there when I arrived, and after we exchanged pleasantries, I told her, "Before we get into the store business, I have to ask you a few questions. There is talk in this restaurant that you did not follow the company policy in regards to not getting involved with an employee; is that correct?" She began to cry and said, "Yes."

Well, that changed everything because our company policy is that a manager will not fraternize with the employees, and it also states, "If a relationship ensues, that manager is immediately to tell his or her supervisor and one of the employees will be transferred to another store; the employees will not work together. If this policy is not followed, the manager may be terminated."

When I asked her whether she knew this policy, she said, "Yes, *but...*" I have to say, if you have to start any sentence with a "but," it's not a good sign. I asked her, "So you know the policy, but because it's you, you don't think it should apply?" Again, "But I love the company. I work hard," and on she went about her dedication, her results, etc. None of those things were even part of our discussion; the bottom line is that everyone must follow the company policy. So without further details, let me just say she is no longer working for the company. Like 99 percent of these situations, this one did not end well. When a coworker shows interest in you, *just say, "No!"* or follow the policy before anything gets started.

I have also seen many women think that the sexual attention they receive from men in power is love; they think, "He must really care about me because he is always calling me, giving me gifts, taking me to nice places, and boy, do I feel special." But let me say that 95 percent of the time, the relationship never goes anywhere except the bedroom, and when you want more than that, the relationship ends. What do you think happens to your job when the relationship ends? Yes, you are right—the job ends too.

Recently, I was watching the movie *Runaway Bride*. As I watched it, my thoughts went to how so many of us think "I'm different; that won't happen to me; I'm not like everyone else." In the movie, every one of the men thought his relationship with the female main character would be different, but guess what—it wasn't. So when you read about how to dress, how to act in the workplace, how you should not get involved with someone at work, and all the other "tips" mentioned in this book, remember—as special as you are, it will happen to you too should you choose to make those poor choices. Treat yourself like your own best friend and always remember people treat you like you let them. Treat yourself with respect and dignity and make sure others treat you the same way.

The takeaway from this chapter is to keep business and personal (romantic) relationships separate. Be known for your talents, your passion, and your desire to achieve work goals. Be a valuable asset to the company and not anything else. Be the woman who gets the next promotion because you are talented and get results.

Lesson #19

BEDROOM VS. BOARDROOM

"Dress shabbily and they remember the dress;
Dress impeccably and they remember the woman."
— Coco Chanel

What looks good in the bedroom doesn't look good in the boardroom. When you are at work, no matter your job, always dress in business and business casual clothes—no exceptions. No sexy clothes, no tight clothes, no very high heels—nothing above 1½ inches—and preferably modest, closed toe shoes; yes, I know open toe shoes are cute, but in business, we're not looking for cute. I do know many, many people who wear them, but you don't need to be one of them. Nothing see-through no matter what. No darker colored items under lighter colored clothes so they show through, and always moderate makeup and jewelry. And leave the perfume for after work.

The bottom line is when we go to work, we always want to be well dressed, but not in a sexy or "notice me" way. Yes, we are women, so yes, we do want to look pretty, but in a business environment we are not looking for sexy, or sleazy. We want to err on the conservative side.

A lot of companies now have "casual day," usually on Fridays. That's great and I know employees love it, but "casual" does not mean sloppy; it's not the day to wear our jeans too tight or our tops too low or tight. Always be the one who sets the best example for everyone in the office, no matter if you're the COO or you work in the mailroom. You never know who is going to see you, and what you wear always is noticed, even when no one says anything.

I've sat in meetings where we've discussed promoting a female employee, but when her name was mentioned, some of the men in the room would laugh and then try to pretend they hadn't; people would then make comments like "She doesn't represent us well." Ouch! That kind of comment is not about her talent or her business skills; it's about the way she conducts herself and the most visible sign of that is how she dresses. Don't be that girl! You've heard the saying, "Dress for the position you want, not the one you have." It's so true! That does not mean you have to shop at an expensive store; it means to wear modest, clean, ironed clothes and look well put together.

If you wonder what exactly is business attire, look around the office. Who do you see who is always well put together? Take some tips from that woman by observing what she wears. If you visit the business dress section of a large department store, the sales staff there can help you put a few outfits together. As females, we all crave attention, but you need to find it outside of work, not at work.

One of the companies I worked at was known for its big company parties, which it held about twice a year. There would be dinner and drinks, and then dancing later for those who wanted to stay and party. I remember attending a meeting where we were discussing the planning for one of these events. One of the men commented, "Be sure the accounting girls are invited because they are so much fun." Of course, all the other men laughed. Yes, the accounting girls did come to the party wearing very short skirts and very high heels, and they drank way too much. Needless to say, they were all the office talked about for the next week. The men should have been embarrassed by the way they flirted and ogled the girls, but they weren't. Actually, it didn't seem like it bothered anyone from the top all the way down.

I didn't feel comfortable with this situation, so when I spoke with the vice president of my department, I expressed my desire not to go to this event because people always ended up drinking too much and doing things they shouldn't be doing. His response to me was "You must attend; if you want to move up the ladder, you have to be seen at all the events." I was smart enough to know he was right, so I told myself, "Okay, I'll go, but I do not have to be part of the late night events. I will be *seen*, but I will leave before the real party gets started."

I learned early on how to handle that situation. Don't be a snob; don't be a goody goody, *but* by no means participate. Be smart—go home alone. I would go, enjoy a nice dinner, and have one drink; then, once the event turned to an out and out party, I left. Not all companies have such parties, but if you work for one that does, I highly recommend you do the same.

Remember, no regrets—be smart and do the right thing. You always want to be known for your work skills and your value to the company, and not for anything else. Let me add that it's a small world; you never know where and when you will work with the same people, where or when you will meet someone who knows you or of you, or someone you know. You want your past to help, not hinder you.

Let me give you an example of how small a world it is and how your past can catch up with you. Recently, I was at a company dinner where we were celebrating our accomplishments, discussing the past year's events, and planning the coming year's goals. I gave my team the opportunity to pick where they wanted to go. They chose a restaurant where, if you made reservations far enough in advance, you could request to sit in the kitchen. That sounds a bit strange, right? But I did tell them it was their choice so reservations were made and that's where we went. We arrived and were escorted to the large table in the kitchen. It was a fun evening, although very different. Right away, we introduced ourselves to the general manager, and we enjoyed the interaction with the cooks, servers, and the management team. I also noticed a gentlemen wearing a shirt and tie who walked by several times, so I engaged him in a conversation; when you've been in the restaurant business for a long time, you can pick out people and most of the time what their position is. He was the Regional VP for the West Coast with this restaurant chain. We talked together about the restaurant, and we all laughed about sitting in the kitchen. He was telling us more about his company when I mentioned a friend of mine who used to work for the company. He asked me who it was, and when I told him, he laughed, picked up his phone, and called him; they were good friends also. See, it is a small world! And now I have a new connection and a person to network with.

So do the right things and it will pay off; you never know whether the next person you meet may offer you your dream job.

Here's another story that didn't end so well. In 1990, there were two restaurant companies that were bought by one large company, and the two of them had to merge and become one company. This created a lot of tension because no one knew who would be keeping their jobs and running this new company. One of the Vice Presidents of Operations had a secretary who was very flirty with everyone; she was an attractive young lady, who was known as being "the party girl" because she enjoyed meeting the guys after work for drinks. At this time, I was a director, and everyone in a position above me was a man and they were all executives who had a secretary or administrative assistant reporting to them, and all of those positions were filled by females. This particular secretary wanted to play with everyone, as well as work for all of them. I will add this group of men was more than willing to participate, and in my opinion, they encouraged this behavior.

Everything went well for this secretary until "Black Friday" came—the term we were using for the day when the decisions would be announced regarding who would be staying to run this new company. The VP to whom this young lady reported was let go that day. When the reorganization was being discussed, the *new* executives mentioned that they had heard enough about this secretary that, although she was good at her job, she was not what they were looking for, so she also was let go. Everyone just credited the reorganization with her dismissal, including her; they were not privy to the inside conversations.

About three years later, we had a few new executives, and some of the previous executives were still there when I heard at a meeting that this female had applied for an administrative position and wanted to come back. Several of the people who were there when she was employed immediately said, "No thank you," so she was not hired. Now who's to say that in those three years, she had not changed? However, because of her previous reputation, they were not willing to give her a job. They did not want the unprofessionalism she and those she worked with were known for.

It is a small world and most executives know each other in our own business world. You may not be known by the executives, but you are known by someone—your managers, directors, and others in your industry. Your reputation will always precede you, so make it a good story to tell, and if you're just starting out, take this lesson to heart. It is so important to ensure your name and your reputation are talked about in high regard, that you are known for your work value, and for your talents at work. You have to help yourself climb the ladder; you have to get on and stay on the right track to continue to move forward.

Lesson #20

HARASSMENT IN THE WORKPLACE

"Trust yourself. Create the kind of self that you will be happy to live with all your life. Make the most of yourself by fanning the tiny inner sparks of possibility into flames of achievement."
— Golda Meir

Harassment in the workplace has several different forms, and it can include bullying as well as sexual harassment. Not only is it men toward women, or women toward men, but it can also be men toward men, and women toward women. In any case, harassment can happen to anyone, and you want to make sure it doesn't happen to you.

The best way to avoid harassment is to focus on work and not on elements outside the workplace. That said, harassment will happen, and it can cause problems not only for those being harassed, but management and a company if the harassment is not handled properly.

If you're in a higher position in a company, make sure you keep open communications at all levels so whenever anyone is feeling uncomfortable or harassed, he or she will feel comfortable about coming to talk to you or the appropriate superior about the situation before the matter gets worse.

When someone brings a harassment situation to your attention, you need to take it seriously. If you do not do anything, you could be held liable because you knew about the situation but did not do anything about it.

One time, I had a sexual harassment incident happen in one of my stores. Sadly, by the time I learned about it, it had been going on for a long time, and one employee quit because of it. The employee being harassed was a twenty-year old male who was living at home, going to school, and working part-time. He was a really good worker, very good at customer service, kept busy all the time, and was a really good trainer for the front of the house.

I found out about this situation one day when I was touring stores, and at one particular store, I noticed that this young man, who had been with the company for two years, was no longer there. When I asked his manager where he was, I was told matter-of-factly, "Oh, he quit." This response did not settle well with me. I could not understand why a really good employee would just quit.

So I asked his manager to step inside the office where I could talk with him privately. Then I probed into what had led up to this employee quitting. The manager said he did not know. He assured me that he had asked the employee several times, but the employee had only continued to say, "I just don't want to work there anymore."

The next day, I had HR bring me the young man's file so I could get his phone number. When I called him, he did not want to tell me any more than he had told his manager, but with my persistence, he agreed to meet with me away from the store. During this meeting, he finally told me there was another male employee who had been sexually harassing him for six months. He had never told anyone because he was embarrassed. The other employee had threatened him, saying he knew he was gay, and if he either didn't go out with him or if he told anyone, he would make sure everyone knew his sexual preference, and that he would tell everyone he was the one being harassed. Sadly, this young man believed the other employee and felt scared for several reasons. He thought the best way he could deal with this "bully" was to leave and never tell anyone.

After we talked for a long time, I assured him that telling me was the best thing he could do. I did not want to lose him as an employee, and I knew he needed to work. I was sorry he didn't feel comfortable enough to tell anyone so we could put a stop to it. Unfortunately, he did not come back to work because he felt too uncomfortable. As for the employee who had been harassing him, he quit when he heard I had made contact with this employee.

So you see, harassment and bullying can happen to anyone. We have to make sure every employee knows there is an "Open Door" policy, and we will not let anyone retaliate against anyone who tells what's happening to him or to anyone else. Working in this business as long as I have, I have had many cases of sexual harassment arise. Most of them have been brought to my attention and were able to be dealt with before they got out of control.

Sadly, when we work in the corporate atmosphere, uncomfortable situations do happen, and most of the time, they go unreported. Too many people in this situation think, "I can handle it," or "If I tell anyone, I'll lose my job or be transferred to another department," or "If I say anything, I won't be promoted *ever*." When people get away with bad behavior, they come to feel it is acceptable for them to behave that way, or at least that they can get away with it. Often they feel untouchable because they are so good at getting results for the company that they think everyone will look the other way.

To avoid being harassed yourself, my best advice to you is to act professionally, dress professionally, and keep your language and conversations professional. Never tease another employee, comment on how he or she looks, or touch him or her—it will never turn out good if you do. Following these simple guidelines will eliminate 80 percent of possible situations; for the other 20 percent, you will need to seek advice from your mentor or someone you trust so you can handle your situation correctly.

Remember, never should you let anyone harass you in the workplace. People treat you the way you let them, so don't let them.

Lesson #21

NO SURPRISES

"The greatest pleasure in life is doing what people say you cannot do."
— Walter Bagehot

One of the first things I teach new managers and employees is that there are three things I will not tolerate in the workplace:

1. Lying
2. Stealing
3. Surprises

Now, you know what lying and stealing are, but you probably wonder what I mean by "surprises."

I mean that you should always be honest and up-front, so if you make a mistake or a bad decision, you need to be the first one to call your boss and tell her. Everyone makes mistakes, but when you do make one, you must own it. One of my favorite sayings is "Do the right thing because it's the right thing to do." If you follow that, you can't go wrong.

You never want your boss to confront you about an issue that your boss had to find out about from someone other than you. Keep your boss informed. Now that you can email, text, and call, there's no reason why your boss should not be informed about issues right away so he can take care of them.

Let me tell you a story of one time when I was caught by surprise and I didn't like it. When I was a director of operations, I had sixteen restaurants and three district supervisors; two of them were responsible for five stores and one for six stores.

One evening, we received a visit from our corporate franchise business coach in our restaurant in Beaumont, California. This visit was not unusual since this person was in our stores often.

On this particular evening, the assistant manager was in charge of the night shift, and of course, it was an evening when someone had called in sick and the assistant manager did not replace that person; the restaurant had a really busy dinner rush, and because of the missing employee, things were not being handled well. The dining room had not been cleaned, and overall, service was slow. All the employees on duty were working as fast as they could, but just not enough people were working.

When the franchise business coach came in, instead of pitching in and helping, she walked around looking mad and making everyone feel worse than they already did. Once the assistant manager had a minute, she and the crew cleaned the store and got things back on track. The franchise business coach then had a conversation with her, telling her about all the things that were not up to standard and that she would be talking with me. Of course, that's what the assistant manager did not want to happen, but although she tried hard to explain her way out of it, obviously, it didn't help.

The assistant manager did not call to forewarn anyone above her about this situation. I think she didn't call anyone because she knew she had made the wrong decision, and now she was worried about what was going to happen. She had worked for us for two years, so she knew all our policies and procedures. This is where my rule "No surprises" comes in; the best thing she could have done at that point was to call her district manager and explain what had happened so the district manager could let me know *before* I was blindsided by the rude email I received the next morning.

I know things happen, but it's how we deal with them that makes all the difference. The first issue was that an employee had called in sick and the assistant manager had not found a replacement or called her general manager to ensure someone would come in to cover that shift. Because she did not follow that procedure, our customers did not get the service they are supposed to get every time they visit our restaurant. This very poor customer service is a violation of our company policy, and the consequences for this violation can result in a write-up or even a termination. This assistant manager soon after had a meeting with her general manager and her district manager and they issued her a write-up, and not because the franchise business coach was there, but for the unacceptable customer service, which was the outcome of her poor business decision. But also for not following our company policy of "No surprises." Everyone in our company knows how important that policy and all policies are, so not to follow them is unacceptable. (Stay tuned for the rest of this story in the next chapter.)

To avoid surprises and make sure the right thing is done the first time around, when I'm talking with an employee who has just been promoted to an entry level manager position, I tell him or her, "When you make a decision, ask yourself what decision you would make if I were standing next to you. If you remember to do that, you will never be too far off from the right decision."

In making the decision, first get all the information you can. You cannot just hear part of the story or know part of the incident; you can't make a good decision with only half of the information. Remember, deal with the facts. In order to make a good decision, you need good, reliable, accurate information.

If you make a decision based on what's best for you or what's best for an employee and not what's best for the business, you will be wrong most of the time. Being a manager, you have to make sure you make the right decision because there is a lot riding on it, and most of the time when you are stumped, you will have someone to call, but occasionally, you will have to make that decision either right on the spot; sometimes, no one above you is available, so it's all up to you. Understand also that *not* making a decision is also a decision. But not making a decision does not relieve you of any responsibility, so no decision means you've chosen just to let things happen, and you have to decide whether that is what's best for the company and the employees.

Lesson #22

THE TWENTY-FOUR-HOUR RULE

"No regrets—life is too short to wake up with regrets.
Love the people who treat you right.
Forget the ones who don't.
Believe everything happens for a reason.
If you get a second chance, grab it with both hands.
If it changes your life, let it.
Nobody said life would be easy,
God just promised it would be worth it."
— Randy Broad

What is The Twenty-Four-Hour Rule? Never react to something that upsets you until you have had twenty-four hours to think about it thoroughly.

For example, if you receive an email that upsets you, whether it's unprofessional or just outright rude, do not reply until you have thought about it for twenty-four hours. There are times in business when we must make an on-the-spot decision, but that is not what I'm talking about here. I'm referring to an incident where you have been blasted by another peer, your boss just criticized you unfairly, or your best employee just gave you notice and you find yourself immediately angry, upset, or shocked by the situation. Don't react right away. An angry response will just make the situation worse. Give yourself time to cool off first.

Once you've had time to think about the situation with a clear mind and not a lot of emotion, you will know how to handle your response professionally. Not only will waiting give you time to cool off, but it also allows you time to collect the facts; do not listen to hearsay, rumors, or someone saying, "I think this is what so-and-so said." Always get *all* the facts to make the best informed decision.

Here's an example: When I was an area director, I had a general manager in training in one of my stores. On the fifth day of her training, I received a call to tell me she did not show up for work. Now, I have a "No call, no show, means you quit" rule, and everyone who works for me knows it. I immediately asked, "Has the training manager called her to make sure she is okay?" For all I knew, she could have been in a car accident or had other extenuating circumstances. I do want to give people the benefit of the doubt.

Upon further investigation, I found out that she had called, but she hadn't called the training manager, who was her boss; instead, she had called the store and spoken to a shift supervisor; she told the shift supervisor that she would be in, but she would be three or four hours late. Hmm, my first thought was, "Why would a general manager think it is okay to call someone other than her boss to say she'll be three or four hours late?" That's not the kind of behavior I will accept from a member of management. So now I had a different problem—not a no call, no show issue, but instead, I had a general manager trainee who thought one week into the job that she could write her own schedule and did not feel she needed to speak to her boss about arriving late. When she did come into work, I had the training manager send her home, and I scheduled a meeting with her for the next morning. During our meeting, it became clear she did not want to work a schedule; she wanted to come and go whenever she wanted, even during training. At that point, I ended our conversation and her employment. Again, getting all the facts is the most important requirement if you want to make the best decision.

The point here is that things are not always as they seem at first; yes, I still did have a problem, but each problem has its own way it needs to be dealt with, and without all the facts, you will make mistakes, and some of those mistakes will not only cost you a lot of money, but they could also cost you your job.

While using the Twenty-Four Hour Rule is very important, trust me, at times it is hard to follow. Let me tell you about a time I failed to follow it. One morning, I arrived at my office and started my day as I do most days with coffee and checking emails. One of the first emails I read was from our franchise business consultant; she worked for the corporate company and was responsible for doing audits in our stores to ensure we were following the corporate standards. The email she sent was to tell me about a visit she had made to one of our stores the night before; she was blasting the assistant manager for some problems she had found at the store. (I told part of this story in the last chapter.)

I am and always have been one who stands up for everyone who works for me—not that everyone always does the right thing; we are human and we make mistakes, but I want my employees to feel not only that they have a boss to answer to, but also that we are on the same team. That said, I realize the corporate franchise business coaches have a job to do, so I never think they should give any of my stores special treatment. I just expect that they will always treat my team with respect, and when discussing any issue with anyone, including myself, they will be professional, tell me the facts, and know at the end of the day that we are all on the same side. I don't want them to feel they are working in a "got you" program; we all want the brand to be successful. And yes, after getting the details of how the store conducted business during the dinner rush, I did understand why she was upset.

After reading the email, I immediately contacted the district manager to get all the details. I also immediately wrote back to the franchise business coach. This immediate response is an example of how I should have waited twenty-four hours before responding, but this time, I did not. I responded with too much passion and I took the email personally—big mistake. I am thankful that no matter how much passion I convey in any email, I never become unprofessional (oh, thank goodness). I did tell her in the email that her approach toward my manager was unprofessional, and that in the future, before she spoke with any of my managers about issues in their stores, she needed to call the manager's supervisor and have him or her present so the three of them could handle any and all operations issues together.

I do think this coach made the issue sound far worse than it actually was, although poor customer service is always bad. In my email response, I asked for a face-to-face meeting the next day. Once we met, she did apologize for her email, and she admitted that she had made the restaurant visit sound like a horrible one when, in fact, while it was not the best one she'd ever had, it definitely had not been so terrible as to be worth getting everyone upset. I, in turn, apologized that our store was not staffed correctly, which led to poor customer service. We both agreed that, going forward, when she has an issue with any of my stores, she would call the supervisor right away and not let things get that bad. I have learned a lot from my mistakes since then, and I am still learning today.

In short, before you react:

1. Remember the Twenty-Four Hour Rule.
2. Get all the facts.
3. Do not be emotional.
4. Handle all issues according to your company's employee manual.

Following these simple steps will ensure that you treat all employees the same. I believe in the motto, "Treat people the way you want to be treated." Remember that saying—it's best always to live by it.

Part 4

AFTER THE JOB *and* BEYOND

Lesson #23

DON'T BURN YOUR BRIDGES

"In order to succeed, your desire for success should be greater than your fear of failure."
— Bill Cosby

Do not burn your bridges. When it comes time to leave your job, make sure you leave on good terms, even when you feel you have not been treated fairly. This advice includes leaving when you've been laid off. Sometimes, companies will bring back laid off employees, but if you were unprofessional when they laid you off, you will not get the opportunity to come back.

A person can ruin her image or "good name" when, the minute she lands a new job, she starts treating people terribly at her current job. Always—and I mean always—give at least a two weeks' notice, and be willing to help fill your position, help hire for your position, and clean up any loose ends before you leave.

Sometimes when you give your notice, an employer will decide to pay you for the two weeks of your notice and release you right then, so make sure you have all your belongings ready to go so you are not caught by surprise.

Also any job that tells you that you need to start right away so you don't have time to give your current employer a two weeks' notice may not be an employer for whom you really want to work. I would not want to hire anyone in any management position if that person did not have the courtesy to give her current employer a two weeks' notice; I figure if the person will do that to her previous employer, she could do it to me as well.

You always want to be eligible for rehire when you leave a job, even if you know you will never want to go back to that company. Just knowing you have that job as a possibility to fall back on can make a difference, and more importantly, future employers will call your former employer for a reference or just to verify employment, and they usually will ask whether you are eligible to be rehired, so leaving on bad terms may follow you and hurt your chances for jobs to come.

Be professional whether you're leaving because you gave notice or the company laid you off or let you go. Everyone will remember that you conducted yourself professionally, and in the long run, you'll feel better about yourself for being professional.

This need to leave on good terms is especially true in today's tough economy. There was a time (years ago) when if you wanted a job, you could have one—that didn't mean you would always get the job you wanted, but there were jobs to be had; that is not the case today. Companies are doing more with less; they have had to because of the recession we have been in since 2007. Call it what you want, companies have been downsized to death, and a lot of companies have closed. The ones still hanging on have to keep costs down so employees wear many hats and are just thankful to have a hat to wear. So keep your job and find another one before you leave. Be willing to do what it takes to help your company survive; whining and complaining about all you have to do is not going to help. When you've had a director's position or above and you lose that job, for whatever reason many companies will think you're overqualified (or even under-qualified) for jobs you think you could do. It is definitely an employer's market now, so be smart, plan ahead, and be willing to learn more; share your knowledge and be an asset to your company. Make sure your company values everything you do; that way, when it is time to downsize, your name won't be first on the list.

Lesson #24

TAKE CARE OF YOURSELF

"Love yourself first, and everything else falls in line. You really have to love yourself to get anything done in this world."
— Lucille Ball

I know we hear it all the time: "Take care of yourself." And I, along with everyone else, know that it is true, important, and necessary, *but* I also know most of us women put ourselves last.

Ladies, since my son is now an adult and I am at a good place in my career, I feel like I'm in a great place to speak from experience. We women are so busy nurturing everyone else in our lives that we do not take care of ourselves the way we should. I can tell you every reason why we should take care of ourselves, and then I can tell you every reason why we don't.

Basically, we know we should find the time to take care ourselves, but then I wonder, "If I take the time for myself, who will do everything else?" No matter how many times I've heard, "You should take care of yourself," I never did see anyone coming over to clean my house, take care of my child, do the grocery shopping, *or* any of the other 100 things on my daily/weekly/monthly "To Do" lists. It especially bothered me that the people who did not have all the things to do that I did were the ones saying it the loudest!

We tend to get sick of hearing what we should do when it doesn't come with answers for how to do it, so then we tune it out. It becomes "Blah, blah, blah..." Not that we don't know that it's important—we just don't see how it is possible. Looking back upon my life, that's exactly how I felt for years. I didn't have the luxury of a nanny, or even a grandparent, sister, or brother who could come over and help. Going to the gym was out; I exercised at home when I could get up earlier than my son. So, how in the world was a single mom, without any family around, without a lot of money, who worked many hours trying to build a career, and who spent every spare minute taking care of her son, going to find any time for herself?

Let me say, ladies, that you don't need to take on all of the world's guilt. You don't have to listen to everyone telling you to: "Do more, be more, look this way, act this way," and on and on and on. Find out who you are, and as you grow, so will your wisdom, your strength in who you are, your confidence, and your knowledge in work and in life.

I often say, "If I knew then, what I know now," and then I laugh because it wouldn't have mattered so much to me then, and even if I could have had that knowledge then, I still needed the wisdom from life experiences to know and be what I am today.

I love the saying, "Be your own best friend" because we know that if we treated ourselves like we would our best friends and if we wanted for ourselves what we would want for our best friends, then WOW, what would our lives look like then?

I am not sad over all that I've been through. Instead, I'm thankful for it—I survived, and it made me stronger, more determined, more compassionate toward others, and overall, a better person. But it also taught me the importance of self-care.

Make sure you use your life lessons positively; let them lift you up and fill you with love, hope, and kindness for others. If you let them make you bitter, then it is a lose-lose for you and for the world. Be all you can be—don't give up, don't give in, and hope, dream, and take people with you as you climb. What I do know for sure is that life is short, so we must make the most of each day. No regrets—when you know better, then do better, and then at the end of each day, when you get ready to sleep, I hope you will think of the day and smile because you were all you could be—you did your best and you are proud of who you are.

During my workout this morning, I was watching an interview with Lebron James. His words really struck a chord with me. He was saying that he didn't want people to compare him to Michael Jordan because he is his own person. Yes, we all know Michael Jordan has been called the best basketball player of all time, and now, Lebron James will also be remembered for his incredible basketball skills and being one of the best players ever, but what really caught my attention about him during this interview was that the interviewer said, "I noticed how happy you are lately; you were engaged with a fan at the last game, you ran on the court and hugged another fan, and you are playing phenomenal basketball. Any correlation?" Lebron replied, "Yes, there is. I am at a great place in my life. I'm more relaxed than ever before, and yes, the happier I am and the more fun I'm having, the better my game." I thought, "That's me. I am at a great place in my life. I love my job, I feel so much more happy from the inside out, and I agree with Lebron that it's a great place to be."

I'm telling you this because I want you to know that yes, the journey is difficult at times—okay, even really hard, and at times, it can feel impossible, but it's not.

DO NOT GIVE UP. DO NOT GIVE IN. YOU CAN DO IT!

It feels incredible to be at a place where you feel good about yourself, you feel proud of yourself, and you feel like you're making a difference. I wish that for you in your career and in your life.

Bonus Section

INTERVIEWS WITH SEVENTEEN SUCCESSFUL WOMEN *and* ONE SUCCESSFUL MAN

BONUS SECTION

I saved the best part for last. One of the most important things you can do is learn from other women who are already successful. Don't be afraid to ask for help and surround yourself with women who are successful or whom you admire. People are known by the company they keep, and it's been said that we are the sum of the five people we spend the most time with, so go out and spend time with successful women. Join their groups, ask them out to lunch, pick their brains, find out their secrets to success, and do the same by helping other women when they ask you for help.

Following are interviews with several women, and one man, whom I have come to admire for their business successes and the integrity they have shown in their careers. I hope you learn as much from them as I have.

Interview #1

JESSICA HIGDON

Direct Selling Entrepreneur

Nina: Thank you, Jessica, for the opportunity to interview you today. How long have you been in the direct selling business?

Jessica: I've been in the direct selling business since 2009. I started fresh out of college.

Nina: Why did you get into this industry?

Jessica: I got into this industry because I couldn't find a job after getting my marketing degree. Everywhere I interviewed, they told me I would make a low hourly wage and wouldn't get a raise for years, and I decided I was easily replaceable in corporate America so it wasn't for me. I wanted to create my own future and my own hours. Bottom line: I hated someone else controlling my future and telling me what to do.

Nina: What advice do you have for women who are considering the direct selling business?

Jessica: My advice for women is to understand that confidence is not something you gain from outside circumstances; it's something you gain from within you. From the moment you wake up in the morning to the moment you go to bed, you can have confidence if you choose to have it; it's just a simple choice. This was the hardest thing for me to learn being a young woman with no prior business experience. I felt like I needed something major to happen in my business to start having success, when in actuality something major would happen in my business if I stayed confident and consistent.

Nina: What is the best part of your job and the worst part?

Jessica: The best part of my job by far for me is creating my own schedule. I love that I can wake up whenever I want, work when I want, and take off when I want. Don't get me wrong; I work very hard, but I love that at the drop of a hat, I can go travel somewhere and not worry about asking permission. The best part of my work is also the worst part. I make my own schedule so sometimes it's difficult to make myself work and stay motivated. Being your own boss takes a tremendous amount of will power, and I can fall behind just like anyone else. In order to keep myself productive, I usually pop in a motivational audio or give myself tasks to complete by the end of the day.

Nina: Why do you think you are so successful?

Jessica: I think I'm so successful because I didn't give up or give myself a way out. You'll hear people who were in direct sales say, "It just didn't work," or "I just didn't have the right system." I never gave myself the option to quit. When you find the right vehicle for you, and it's the right timing in your life, you keep going and going until it works. I remember crying in the bathroom so my husband wouldn't see me because I was so frustrated; nothing I was doing seemed to be working. And then all of a sudden, I found a few key leaders to work with and run with my business, and from that point forward, I realized it's simply a numbers game and you can never quit. People don't fail in network marketing; they quit. My advice for anyone looking to pursue this industry would be to stick with something you are passionate about and enjoy, and work with it until you see success. Most successful men and women in direct sales have been with their companies for years and years; there's a reason for that.

Interview #2

PATRICK SNOW

Publishing Coach and Best-Selling Author of *Creating Your Own Destiny* and *The Affluent Entrepreneur*

As I write this book, I am constantly scanning the marketplace to find out what other successful business owners are doing to market themselves better. I have learned from my publishing, speaking, and book marketing coach, Patrick Snow, that we constantly need to test and measure, and learn through trial and error. That means that as we implement new strategies to grow our business, we need to ask ourselves, "Is our strategy working?" If so, we need to do more of it; if not, we should avoid spending more money on marketing ideas that prove to be unprofitable.

For this reason, I recently interviewed my coach so his advice could help you succeed better in business. I know that I wrote this book primarily for woman, but as you will read in Patrick Snow's responses below, these strategies work for both men and women. Patrick is a free-enterprise advocate, and he has been a successful entrepreneur his whole life, dating back to the seventh grade when he earned $80 per night selling *Detroit Free Press* subscriptions door-to-door. Today, Patrick is a professional keynote speaker, publishing coach, and the international best-selling author of *Creating Your Own Destiny* and *The Affluent Entrepreneur*.

Patrick shared with me some insights for his next book soon to be published in which he covers sixteen strategies that all business owners can do to succeed in business. Here is his list of sixteen strategies to drive revenue to your business, which are explained in more detail in our interview below:

1. Give away free samples
2. Allow clients to pay via barter
3. Don't take rejection personally
4. 3XT + 3XM = 30X ROI (Return on Investment)
5. Sales success formula
6. The Rule of Seven
7. The 50 Percent Rule
8. Walk a mile in your prospect's shoes
9. Marketing instead of advertising
10. Use a revenue war board
11. Adding value to the marketplace
12. Leveraging time and technology
13. Do events
14. Publish your book
15. Focus on your business vision
16. Connect with prospects

Nina: Thank you, Patrick, for agreeing to do this interview with me. First, tell me about your first strategy of using **Free Samples.**

Patrick: Successful companies market new products by giving free samples to prospects. This is a strategy the Fortune 500 companies have been using for years.

Not too long ago, our mailboxes were inundated with a 30-Day Free Trial for AOL.com offering a CD to install to sample AOL's Internet service. In more recent times, Gatorade gave away hundreds of thousands if not millions of bottles of its new G2 "diet Gatorade" that we could all sample before making the purchase. As a result, G2 is now just as much a popular drink as regular Gatorade. In my publishing business, I have given away approximately 5,000 copies of my book, *Creating Your Own Destiny*. As a result, I have sold more than 150,000 copies in five languages and in 108 countries. In my coaching business, I have given away more than 2,000 hours of my time by offering complimentary publishing coaching consultations. As a result, I have built a coaching clientele of about 500 or so authors, all because I let people sample my services first for free, with no obligation. If you want to succeed in business, you too must give your prospects the ability to sample your product or service without making an investment. If they like it, they will flat out invest in you or in your product or service. Side note: Make sure you use terms like "complimentary" instead of "free." Complimentary shows value, but free is cheap.

Nina: Next talk about why you feel that **Bartering** is so important.

Patrick: The bottom line is that not every one of your prospects is going to be flush with cash, or have available room on their credit. Therefore, we as business owners need to be able to accept clients who pay by cash, check, credit cards, or bartering for what they offer. For example, on several occasions I have had potential clients who had their cash flow tied up in other things, so they simply could not afford to pay cash, check, or use credit card to invest in my publishing coaching services. So in these cases, I got creative and I asked them what did they have that they no longer needed or would be willing to part with in order to invest in my coaching. I was shocked with the results. One guy gave me a week's stay at his timeshare in Hawaii for our family and two friends. Another guy gave me the title to his 1968 Ford Mustang, which I later traded for a Porsche 944 Turbo (since I am more of a Porsche than a Mustang guy), and finally, a third gave me the title to her BMW motorcycle, which I sold on Craigslist and turned into cash. My point is that you need to be flexible and accept whatever the prospect is willing to pay both in the amount of the sale, and in the currency or bartered item he has in mind. When you do that, you will experience some pretty amazing perks, increase your reviews, and pick up more clients as a result.

Nina: Tell me more about **Not Taking Rejection Personally.**

Patrick: One of the most important lessons I have learned in business is that some people are going to like you, some people aren't, so what, next, someone else is waiting. I call this SW4 (some will, some won't, so what, next, someone else will buy from you). One of my all time favorite mentors, speakers, and authors, Les Brown, taught me "Never let someone else's opinion of you determine your reality." My goal has always been and will always be to find 100 people (or organizations) to say "No" to me. The reason is…if I can find 100 people to say "No" then I am sure I will earn 30-40 sales somewhere along the line. Another of my mentors, Brian Tracy, taught me that if you want to earn $1M per year, then you must go out there and get ten prospects to tell you "No" by 9 a.m. each morning. If you do that, then you will successfully earn $1 million per year. The problem is that most people are not willing to do this. Furthermore, most will never set themselves up to get 10 "No's" in a month, and some not in a year. For this reason, they will suffer for a lifetime with "under-earner's disease." Of course, this is not what I want for you. Grow a thick skin, never take rejection personally, shoot for 100 "No's," and in doing so, you will become an unstoppable force of power capable of creating your own destiny!

Nina: Tell me about your **3XT, 3XM=30X ROI.**

Patrick: A successful business takes three times the money and time, but equals 30 times the investment. The bottom line is that the old saying, "Nothing ventured, nothing gained," is true and so is "It takes money to make money." I guess if I have learned anything in business, it is that building a successful business is like building a home; it always costs more than you budget, and always takes longer than you anticipate. Therefore, to succeed in business, my formula teaches you that you should allocate three times as much time as you hope it will take and allocate three times as much money as you ideally want to invest. As a result, if you can survive the 3X time, and 3X money, you will experience up to 30X greater the income than you ever made working as an employee. For this reason, I believe that being an entrepreneur is without question the absolutely best career in America today! Most people aren't willing to sacrifice this investment of time and money, and consequently, most will be stuck in a dead end job their entire lives, living in mediocrity. This is not what I want for any of you reading this book!

Nina: Tell me more about this **Sales Success Formula.**

Patrick: I believe friends buy from friends and people buy from whom they know, like, and trust. Therefore, instead of looking at your prospects as simply having dollar signs on their heads, you need to focus on developing relationships. To do this, over time you need to build trust and respect, qualify your prospects' needs, and then finally ask them for their business. The formula is as follows:

Trust + Respect + Need + *Asking* = The $ale (T+R+N+A=$)

One of my mentors taught me to A-S-K if you want to G-E-T! If you don't ask, you won't get. I firmly believe that this formula is the single great equation that all business owners must follow if they are to maximize their revenues. This brings us to the next point.

Nina: What is the **Rule of Seven**?

Patrick: In Napoleon Hill's book, *The Law of Success*, he has determined that on average it takes seven bits of communication between buyer and seller to close the sale. I certainly believe this to be true, so as a result, I am constantly trying to communicate with my prospect seven times as quickly as possible (perhaps over the course of a few days or a few weeks). However, a big mistake many business owners make is that they are constantly attempting to use the "one call close," and in today's environment, it simply does not work. There is one exception to this, and that is if a girl scout shows up at your door selling cookies. This is the only organization in the world that I know which is successful with a one call close. For all the rest of us, in order for us to acquire new business, we must meet with, speak with, and communicate via email with our prospects upwards of seven times. When we do so, more times than not, you will close the sale and earn more business.

Nina: Tell me then what **The 50 Percent Rule** is all about?

Patrick: Let's face it; today's small business owners are the CEOs of their own companies, and the janitors. We are the VP of Sales and the Director of Customer Service. We are the Accounts Payable Manager and the Operations Manager. Bottom line, we wear multiple hats in our companies and play numerous roles. Therefore, as a result of having our time pulled in every direction, we often lose sight of the number one most important goal of any and all companies, which is to earn a profit. As a result, the 50 Percent Rule is all about making certain that small business owners spend 50 percent of their working hours wearing the VP of Sales hat and spend a minimum of 50 percent of their working hours prospecting for new clients. When we do that, we will see revenues continue to climb. Conversely, when we get stuck in the administrative role of email, voicemail, etc., we slowly but surely go broke. Therefore, moving forward, do not count the number of calls you make, but rather keep track of making sure that you spend 50 percent of your time prospecting. When you do this, your revenues will soar.

Nina: What do you mean when you say, **"Walk a mile in your prospect's shoes"**?

Patrick: The problem with business today is that often business owners see each other as nothing more than prospects with dollar signs on their foreheads, and they don't see each other as human beings with issues and challenges just like the rest of us. Everyone has "stuff" going on in his or her mind. It could be caring for an aging parent, the loss of a loved one, or a relationship ending badly, perhaps even financial challenges. Therefore, as business owners, we need to step outside of our shoes, go over and step into the shoes of our prospects, and as a result, we can feel their pain, understand their challenges, and finally empathize with them. By doing so, you will have a far greater chance of bringing on a new client. As an example, Subway once paid me $15,000 to do a keynote speech at its international conference of franchise owners in Chicago. I accepted this engagement only on the condition that they allow me to volunteer during a four-hour lunch shift so I could actually work at a Subway restaurant baking break, making sandwiches, and baking cookies. They said I was the first speaker in twenty years of booking speakers ever to do such a thing. As a result, I came to understand firsthand that their business is not about making sandwiches; it is about taking the youth of today (their workers), and helping them become the leaders of tomorrow. I shared this message with them, and because I walked a mile in their shoes, I got a standing ovation and a follow-up booking. If you do the same, you will be amazed with your results.

Nina: Why is focusing on **Marketing instead of Advertising** so important?

Patrick: Consumers today are bombarded with advertisements that we simply just do not believe. However, when we watch TV, read the newspaper, or listen to the radio, we still believe the article, the TV show, or the interview, but we tune out all the ads in between. As a result, advertising is very, very expensive, and most of the time, it does not work. Whereas marketing is less expensive (and sometimes even free) and works virtually all the time. On December 5th, 2002, lots of people took out ads in *USA Today*, but I suspect most of them did not pick up new clients as a result. I, on the other hand, was fortunate enough to be featured as a cover story in that issue, and I have gotten lots and lots of mileage out of the article ever since, netting me lots of new speaking and publishing clients. Therefore, my challenge to you is to market your business and quit wasting your money on advertising it!

Nina: Tell me about a "**Revenue War Board**?"

Patrick: In war and business, you need to have a plan of attack. In business, this means you have to know who you are calling on and what revenues are coming in the door to keep your lights on, so to speak. Therefore, I recommend you get a white war board for you office wall and list all prospects on it along with the total dollar value they represent. On my war board, I have my annual income goal, my monthly income goal, the gap on month to date (MTD) and year to date (YTD). I update my prospect list on my war board at the end of every month and numerous times during the month. The great thing about having this displayed in your office is that you will always know whom to call on next. Often, we will have a phone appointment cancel and then we are unsure what to do. Whenever this happens to me, I simply look at my revenue war board to see whom I have not communicated with in several weeks, and then I call that person. A revenue war board is a very productive tool and one that will allow you to double or triple your income in the years to come.

Nina: How can one **Add Value to the Marketplace**?

Patrick: Last year, I earned an extra $75,000 in income on this principle alone. I once heard that if you are not completely happy with the level of your income, then *you* are the only one to blame! This principle just means that you are not adding enough value to the marketplace. Simply put, increase your value to others and your income will increase by the same proportion! In my situation as a publishing coach, I offered one publishing mastermind call per week to all of my 400 plus clients. It is (and still is) every Monday morning at 8 a.m. However, I realized with this principle that due to working requirements, some of my clients were not able to attend this call because they are at work at this time. Therefore, I realized that if I increased my group coaching calls from one per week to now doing a daily M-F 12 noon call, I would then offer six calls per week where my clients could dial in; then I would add six times that value to my clients, and now they could all speak with me live every single weekday. Better yet, those who worked in corporate

America could still dial in on their lunch hours. If you want to increase your income, I challenge you to brainstorm more ways that you and your business can add more value to your prospects and customers. This year, I have decided to write forewords for all my clients who are interested in having my foreword in their book, as yet another way to add more value.

Nina: Tell me how one can **Leverage Time and Technology** to get ahead in business.

Patrick: This kinds of ties into the previous point above. Prospects often ask me how in the world do I give all 500+ of my clients the adequate individual time they need so they can properly write and publish a book? My secret is to leverage both time and technology. Therefore, of course, I do one-on-one coaching with my clients, but I don't think that is enough. My clients all want to meet my other clients who are also going through the process of writing and publishing a book, and when they meet, they often create long-lasting friendships as a result. Therefore, I leverage technology by doing six conference calls per week. During my Monday call, I regularly have thirty clients on the line. So I give up one hour of my time making these calls, and in doing so, I provide thirty hours of coaching to thirty clients. Additionally, I host a Best Seller Publishing Institute four times per year. Two in Hawaii and two in Washington. Typically, this conference is a twenty-five hour event over three days, and we average thirty people in attendance. So I am giving up twenty-five hours of my time, and in return, giving 750 hours of coaching. These are two examples of how you too can leverage both time and technology.

Nina: Why are **Doing Events** so important?

Patrick: One of my mentors, Bob Mowad, always said, "*When I speak, business happens!*" What he means is that every time we do a workshop, seminar, or speech, we set ourselves up for bringing on new business. This additional exposure gives more people the opportunity to learn about our business in a low-pressure environment. So as a result of speaking (whether you are being paid to speak or not), you will get more speaking, coaching, and consulting opportunities. It does not matter the size of the audience; for example, one time I planned on hosting a publishing seminar, but when it came down to doing the event, I only had one RSVP. Initially, I thought about cancelling, but I remembered Bob's words, "When I speak, business happens" and proceeded with the seminar. When I showed up, the attendee immediately whipped out his Visa card, invested $4,000 in my coaching services, and then got a one-on-one coaching session from me for the next 2.5 hours. This experience reinforced the importance of consistently doing events, big or small; it doesn't matter. Every time you speak, you are putting yourself out there and preparing your bank account for more revenue.

Nina: Tell my why **Publishing Your Book** is what you call "The World's Greatest Marketing Secret."

Patrick: Every human being on the planet is an expert at whatever in life he or she is most passionate about. However, unless you have the word "author" next to your name, no one gives you any respect for what you know, and it is virtually impossible to get any publicity from the media. When you write and publish your book, you are announcing to the world that you are indeed an expert and you are communicating this expertise to the media and your prospects. Once you have your book published and in hand, the goal then needs to be to get as many copies of your book as you can into the hands of all your prospects. A book is a lead-generating tool, a fat business card, and a physical website. When you give your book away to your prospects, you set yourself apart from all the others vying for their business. Simply put, I don't know of a better marketing strategy known to man that will boost your business and revenues better than positioning your book to drive revenue to your bank account.

Nina: Tell me more about the importance of **Focusing on Your Business Vision.**

Patrick: I find that people too often (and especially small business owners) constantly get stuck with worrying about the "how" in terms of "how" they will drive revenue and achieve their goals. It is my belief that you have no reason to worry about the how until you come to own your vision. One of my mentors taught me that once you come to taste your vision, smell your vision, touch your vision, emotionalize your vision, and finally, OWN your vision, then the "how" will slowly present itself over time. W. Clement Stone said: *"If you want something bad enough, tell enough other people what it is that you want and sooner or later something or someone will show up in your life and help you get it!"* A favorite quote I learned many years ago says this, *"Only those who can see the invisible can achieve the impossible; the belief in your vision holds the key to creating your own destiny."*

Therefore, I am a big proponent of creating a vision board with images of your goals, and then as your mind sees those goals on a regular basis, you let your subconscious mind come to believe in them; as a result, all things in the universe will conspire on your behalf to help your visions become real.

Nina: Finally, Patrick, tell me what you mean when you say **Connect with Prospects**?

Patrick: The challenge that many salespeople and small business owners have is that they fail to make a connection with their prospects. This connection process may be the difference between whether they do business with you. Therefore, always remember that: Instead of selling, serve! Instead of marketing, connect. This is a secret for succeeding in business. When you focus on serving and connecting, you will literally be amazed with the results.

• • •

Thank you, Patrick, for this fantastic interview!

Now for those of you reading this book, I challenge you not to read Patrick's interview just once, but to read it again and again, and most importantly, apply this knowledge to your business so you can succeed and achieve your goals.

Interview #3

KRISTEN SNIDER

Senior Operations Leader with YUM Brands

Nina: Hi, Kristen. Thank you for agreeing to do this interview. What is your current position?

Kristen: Senior Operations Leader.

Nina: How did you decide this is the career you wanted? Can you give me some details about your career from its beginning until now?

Kristen: When I was deciding on a career path, I took into consideration my strengths and weaknesses as a person. I wanted to make money and do something that was "high-achieving," but I knew I was not cut out to be a doctor (never very strong in sciences and a little squeamish), and I didn't want to be a lawyer (came from a family of lawyers and didn't want any part of that). I was okay at math, but not at the level where I could be an engineer…and I like to talk to people. So, business to me seemed to be a great place for a well-rounded, social person with a lot of drive who enjoyed competition.

So, I set out on a path to achieve the highest position I could possibly achieve. Although the companies and the industries in my career have changed through the years, my overall path and goal remains the same. I started working for Altria Group in college, working full-time while going to school for my B.S. They approached me with an internship that was more than copying papers or running errands, so I saw a huge opportunity to grow professionally in that organization. I worked on special projects for them like pricing strategy and promotions/consumer behavior analysis. They offered me a full-time position after my summer internship, so I continued with them through the rest of college, worked for them post-grad in sales and marketing for seven years and achieved two more promotions during that time. I had the opportunity to manage people and a sales team, and I found it very rewarding and wanted to continue on that path. Altria paid for my master's degree, so I went back to my alma mater USC and received my MBA in 2005.

Upon completing my degree, I took a job with Pepsi in sales, with the promise that they would allow me the opportunity to advance my career at an accelerated rate. I fast-tracked with them for the next seven years, and I had a total of nine jobs with them in those seven years. In my last position, I led a team of sales managers specifically focused on our restaurant sales (contracts and operations management with restaurants) which then segued to my current position in restaurant operations with Yum Brands. So, long story, but it illustrates the point. My career decision has been largely based on partnering with organizations that can grow my career so I can achieve my ultimate goal of being a CEO.

Nina: As you look back over your career, what is the one thing you learned that you would like to share with other women?

Kristen: Be yourself and choose a career that makes you happy; one that is fulfilling and maximizes your personal strengths. When we are being our true selves, and we are truly happy and rewarded by our careers, it is infectious. Work never feels like work, and those around you can pick up on it too, so results tend to follow almost organically. We only get one life to live on this planet, and consciously making decisions that promote happiness are so important to a successful life. It sounds easy in theory, but so many of us get stuck in obligations or emotional baggage that prevent us from making decisions that promote our life rather than detract from it.

Nina: If you could do one thing over in your business career, what would that be?

Kristen: This is a tough one…I don't really regret anything I have done career-wise, but I do wish I had perhaps treated people with more respect and kindness early in my career. I was a bit of a firecracker, but in some ways, it saved me from the "soft" stereotype that we women sometimes get in business.

Nina: Why do you feel you are successful?

Kristen: Two reasons:

1. I work really hard and make decisions that promote my ultimate goal. Faced with a career decision, my

choices have always been based on whether or not it moves my career forward.

2. Other people who sponsored me. There are two parts to this...people can't just sponsor you for no reason, right? It has to be earned through: 1) Actual results and efforts that *must* be communicated, and 2) Developing relationships with people who have been able to support me through my career (managing up).

Nina: How much time do you spend networking?

Kristen: Every day. I make a conscious effort to call or connect with at least three people who are career-supporters every day.

As far as networking events...like big productions with groups of people, about once a month.

Nina: For a female who is either starting or rejoining the business world, what advice would you give her?

Kristen: Choose something you have an interest in, that you enjoy, and that makes you happy...and if you don't know what that is, take the time, do some soul-searching, and write down your strengths and weaknesses, and what you like (very generally), and figure it out. You'll work harder and it will be much more fulfilling than feeling forced into going to a job every day.

Nina: What has been your greatest obstacle in your career?

Kristen: The glass ceiling. The good-old boys' network.

Nina: How did you overcome that obstacle?

Kristen: Not thinking of myself as an outsider, being approachable, and consciously making a decision to get a "coach" or friend on the inside of that network. I think at any level, a lot of success internally in an organization comes from having the respect of and a relationship with not only your peers, but those above you. It has to be easy for them to want to do business with you, and they have to respect your work. Outlining my successes in a factual way (promoting myself) has been something I have worked on over time… and I think men sometimes do better than women in promoting themselves and celebrating their successes.

Nina: Given a platform to speak to women, is there anything else you would like to say to them?

Kristen: Not only in business, but in life: What you give out, you get back. Believe in yourself.

Interview #4

BETTY CAMARILLO

Director of Human Resources for Little Caesar Enterprises, Inc.

Nina: Thank you, Betty, for this interview. What is your current position?

Betty: Director of Human Resources for Ilitch Holdings; Little Caesar Enterprises, Inc.

Nina: How did you come to the decision that you wanted a career in human resources? Can you give me some detail about your career from its beginning until now?

Betty: I decided that I wanted to combine the field of human resources with my education and training in order to utilize the skills I had acquired in all three disciplines to impact the people I work with and come into contact with.

I began babysitting and teaching at twelve years old; part of babysitting was playing games and entertaining young children of different ages. As a young Sunday school teacher, I was responsible for teaching a weekly lesson to a group of young children.

I worked my way through college by teaching swimming and diving lessons and coaching swim teams of children and young adults. Upon graduation from the University of Arizona, I began teaching and coaching junior high school, high school, and community college students.

Having teaching, training, and development success with people of different ages and socio-economic backgrounds and cultures provided a strong foundation for my growth and career journey.

During my ten-year teaching career, I completed a bachelor and two master's degrees in secondary education, education administration, and counseling and guidance. I used these skills to transition into training and human resources in the hospitality and service industry; Disneyland Hotel, PepsiCo; Kentucky Fried Chicken, Columbia Savings and Loan, Baskin Robbins, Baskin Robbins 31 Flavors, Del Taco, Boot Barn, Mancha Development, and Ilitch Holdings—Little Caesar Enterprises, Inc.

During my continuing education career journey, I have completed a Certificate of Business from the School of Business from the University of Southern California, a Certificate of Human Resources from Chapman College, a Law Certificate from the Institute of Applied Management and Law, a Certificate from OSHA, an Honorary Doctorate from the Culinary Art Institute, as well as attending classes from EEOC, Business Labor Relations Institute, and other HR applicable courses. During this time, I also served as President of the Council of Hotel and Restaurant Trainers for two terms as well as serving on its board for another eleven years. In addition, I have represented Ilitch Holdings at California Employment Law Council (CELC) quarterly meetings, and most recently, I have been asked to participate as a CELC board member, which I declined due to other commitments.

Nina: As you look back over your career, what is the one thing you learned that you would like to share with other women?

Betty: I have traveled a very exciting career path, and I have learned that a woman must be true to herself. She needs to take the time to assess who she is, what are her strengths and weaknesses, be comfortable in saying, "Yes" and stepping into the unknown. Being strong and confident in yourself will provide an opportunity to learn something new, meet someone new, and grow. That is exciting and it should never end!

Nina: If you could do one thing over in your business career, what would that be?

Betty: If I could do one thing over in my business career, I would have accepted the offer from Unocal to transfer to Phoenix to Tosco, the acquiring company, in order to go international and travel and train franchisees in the Asian Pacific countries.

At the time, due to family obligations, I chose to stay in California and not accept the offer. I missed not having the international experience.

Nina: Why do you feel you are so successful?

Betty: I feel I am very successful because my journey and life have not always been easy for me. I understand people, and I am caring and compassionate and enjoy working with them; they inspire and motivate me.

Everyone is unique, and I try to identify that unique trait to work more closely with people.

Nina: How much time do you spend networking?

Betty: Networking has been a critical component of my life. It is ongoing, beginning with classmates I went to school with and people I have worked with and associated with throughout my career.

Nina: For a female who is either starting or rejoining the business world, what advice would you give her?

Betty: A female starting or rejoining the world of work will want to make sure she is current on her position and career in relation to our changing world. Yes, that is huge, but she must be knowledgeable and flexible to understand the current and future implications in order to add value to her company.

Nina: What has been your greatest obstacle in your career?

Betty: I have defined "career" as my journey through the world of work. Because of the economy, I have experienced buying and selling and company mergers and have been a part of these changes and transitions. As a result, I have experienced "a long-term relationship with one company."

Nina: How did you overcome that obstacle?

Betty: I found "the obstacle" of being, bought, sold, or merged to be very exciting. As a part of change, I was on the front of growth and development in a variety of industries. I kept my focus on contributing and being flexible to work through transitions.

Nina: Given a platform to speak to women, is there anything else you would like to say to them?

Betty: Be aware of a company's strategic plan, goals, and objectives in order to be a contributing member and to add value.

If it is your company, you want to make sure you have communicated and live your life so your employees know that you "walk the talk." Set the example.

As a woman in the business world, you can best serve yourself and the company you work for by being strong and confident in everything you do.

Your core values are critical; be true to yourself and your reputation and stay the course. Your actions will speak for themselves.

Interview #5

MYRNA SCHULTZ

Vice President of Marketing for Strategic Restaurants

Nina: Thank you, Myrna, for agreeing to do this interview. What is your current position?

Myrna: Vice President of Marketing and Development.

Nina: How did you come to the decision that you wanted a career in marketing and development? Can you give me some details about your career from the beginning until now?

Myrna: I was one of those driven kids who "knew what they wanted to be when they grew up," and I chose my college based on it having a school in advertising/marketing. I received my undergraduate degree in advertising (and statistics) and graduate business degree. I was recruited into Leo Burnett advertising in Chicago in strategic planning and account management, and after two years, I joined the "client side" at Clorox in brand management. I consulted after that for ad agencies and packaged goods companies, and then I joined Wells Fargo Bank in its Internet banking division, working on then start-up companies such as eBay and Amazon. A friend called about a job at a restaurants franchise with an equity stake. Four years in, I was given added responsibility for development and construction.

Nina: As you look back over your career, what is the one thing you learned that you would like to share with other women?

Myrna: To help people to showcase their talents and promote success.

Nina: If you could do one thing over in your business career, what would that be?

Myrna: Stay at an ad agency longer to learn media.

Nina: Why do you feel you are so successful?

Myrna: I knew what I wanted early on, am very driven and focused, asked a lot of questions, and I love what I do.

Nina: How much time do you spend networking?

Myrna: Not enough. Maybe fifty hours annually.

Nina: For a female who is either starting or rejoining the business world, what advice would you give?

Myrna: Learn current technology and trends, and showcase your background and talents.

Nina: What has been your greatest obstacle in your career?

Myrna: Desiring to have a life! Not being willing to relocate for a job.

Nina: How did you overcome that obstacle?

Myrna: By learning to be happy with my success in work and life.

Nina: Given a platform to speak to women, is there anything else you would like to say to them?

Myrna: Help your fellow peers to succeed.

Interview #6

BRENDA HELPS

Senior Vice President of Human Resources and Organizational Development for Miraval Resorts

Nina: Thank you, Brenda, for agreeing to be interviewed. What is your current position?

Brenda: I am currently in transition, after my position was eliminated in January 2013. My last role was Senior Vice President of Human Resources & Organizational Development for Miraval Resorts.

Nina: How did you come to the decision that you wanted a career in human resources, and once you decided HR was where you wanted to be, why did you decide to move up the corporate ladder?

Brenda: I entered the field of HR in the early ’90s, which isn’t all that long ago, but it’s funny now to think back on how I was encouraged by mentors and senior colleagues to pursue a role in HR because it was a field that held “lots of opportunities for women.” We now think of it as a field that is ripe with opportunities for people vs. being a profession primarily for women.

I had been working in an operations position and was tapped to assist the company with a standardization project that was housed out of the HR department. The project evolved into a full-time role involving the training of operational service standards, which later evolved into a training director position and later exposed me to all generalist functions in the realm of HR.

I have always worked in service environments and was attracted to this industry because I enjoyed interacting with guests and making a difference in people's days and in how they experienced whatever brand I worked for. I recognized that in HR I had the same opportunities to impact people in a positive way, but the opportunities were even more meaningful because of the long-term relationships I could build with co-workers.

I have been lucky to have always aligned myself with growing organizations. I don't remember ever setting a specific goal for myself to move up and become an HR executive necessarily, but I have always had a desire to expand my learning and grow my skill set by expanding my responsibilities, and I'm grateful that I've been provided with the avenues to take on bigger positions.

Nina: As you look back over your career, what is the one thing you learned that you would like to share with other women?

Brenda: Be like bamboo: bend, but don't break! Learn to be adaptable. If there is one constant in business and in life, it's that things are going to change. The more one can strengthen one's ability to roll with change rather than resist it, the better off she will be in all aspects of her life and career. Given the dynamic conditions that most businesses have to operate under in today's world, it's an asset for any company to have people who can easily alter priorities and fluidly shift their direction.

Nina: If you could do one thing over in your business career what would that be?

Brenda: About ten years into my career, I started keeping a daily journal. Not just a list of tasks and to-do's, but an actual log of what I was learning along the way, a record of questions I sought the answers to and observations I made about the teams and individuals I worked with. So many valuable insights can be found when you go back and review what you've written down, whether at the end of the day, or months or even years later. I wish I had started this practice earlier.

Nina: Why do you feel you are so successful?

Brenda: I am an excellent listener with a high level of emotional intelligence. I have found this attribute to be more and more critical as my career has progressed because each organization I've been associated with has been focused on people, with its success dependent upon many diverse individuals working in synergy. Because I place value on making an effort to understand the needs, wants, and emotions of my co-workers, and because I make an effort to be constantly aware of how my own needs, wants, and emotions impact the interactions I have with them, it is easy for me to get along with others. I believe that when harmony exists, unnecessary conflict and distractions are eliminated and more work gets done.

Nina: How much time do you spend networking?

Brenda: I spend 1 ½ hours per week of formal networking through a women's organization I belong to, plus a monthly luncheon with a second organization, plus a few conferences per year. But I believe a person can and should network anytime, anywhere…at parties, in line at Starbucks, while getting your hair done, etc. And the power of networking through social media can't be ignored, either.

Nina: For a female who is either starting or rejoining the business world, what advice would you give her?

Brenda: Position yourself as a problem solver vs. a problem creator. I see this as a mindset rather than a skill or ability. Work at having a naturally positive outlook, beginning with an intrinsic belief that there's a reasonable solution for every challenge, and make this your consistent approach. Everyone can work proactively to shape her personal environment based on her goals, which means she can also be successful in shaping an organization, based on its goals.

Nina: What has been your greatest obstacle in your career?

Brenda: In the past, human resources was commonly perceived as a "fluff" department that didn't produce the same level of contribution and, therefore, it wasn't held in the same esteem as marketing, finance, operations, etc.

Nina: How did you overcome that obstacle?

Brenda: I realized that my colleagues in other divisions didn't fully understand what was happening in HR, and therefore, they couldn't connect how HR impacted the big picture. I worked hard to quantify continuously what I achieved in my division. I developed benchmarks and metrics and made sure that my colleagues were not only aware of the targets my team and I were striving for, but I also involved them in developing new targets that we could achieve together. I earned a seat at the table by becoming a strategic business partner with the other divisions, successfully transforming a "support" department into an internal consultancy.

Nina: Given a platform to speak to women, is there anything else you would like to say to them?

Brenda: Some believe that working in a heartfelt way means you're soft, or that you openly display your weaknesses. That isn't the case. Smart organizations value authenticity and heartfelt leadership because the highest levels of achievement in service and performance only come when the hearts of employees are engaged. Working in a heartfelt way means honoring people for the individuals they are. It means truly believing in what the company stands for, being consistent in words and actions, being humble in admitting mistakes, and being as transparent as is reasonably possible. This is what builds trust among coworkers, and it is critical because you must first touch a heart before you can effectively ask for a hand.

Interview #7

NANCY TAYLOR

Zone Leader for 7-Eleven

Nina: Thank you, Nancy, for agreeing to this interview. What is your current position?

Nancy: My current position is Zone Leader of Northern California and Nevada for 7-Eleven, Inc.

Nina: Tell me about your career from its beginning until now?

Nancy: I began my career in Quick Service, thinking I just needed a job now to strategize for the career I really wanted. Little did I know that working at Wendy's would be fun, very interesting, and fraught with challenges since I had never before managed people. At the time, Wendy's Corp. had recently acquired restaurants from a franchisee. Our goals were simply to ensure procedures and sales increases.

During the two years I worked for Wendy's, I moved through two levels of being an assistant manager and then was promoted to restaurant manager all within ten months of my starting with the company. I would like to say it was because I was so impressive, but the reality was quite different. We were scheduled a minimum of fifty-five hours per week, working six-day weeks, and in many cases, to get the seventh day off, you had to work an "open to close" the day before your day off. You can only imagine how high the company's total turnover was at the time. What that experience did teach me, though, is that to be successful, you have to understand and know your business, but you also have to value who you are, what you enjoy, and create a passion for what you do. If I had not enjoyed what I was doing, I never could have survived.

After a couple of years, I looked around and only found one female district manager in the company—not very good odds for future promotions. Burger King Corp. started opening company restaurants in and around Phoenix so I made the move. Initially hired as an assistant manager, I soon moved to being a restaurant manager, then became a troubleshooter in and around Phoenix. During my time at Burger King Corp., I was fortunate enough to help open restaurants in Europe with AAFES, move through various HR/training positions, and become a franchise business consultant. Ultimately, I learned many of the business operations of restaurants from the different perspective of each of these positions.

Next, I jumped into a partnership with an existing Burger King franchise group as a franchisee/director of operations. Looking back on my decisions, I see I had become enamored with the idea of being a business owner, but not necessarily with the processes themselves. In the first year, we acquired fourteen Hardee's restaurants, converting them into Burger Kings and we built one from the ground up. During that time, I learned several lessons that have continued to help me in my career. First, always have a Plan B, C, and D. I know in our culture that concept has almost become a joke, but in business, if we don't have fall-back plans on real-life execution of Plan A, how do you readjust? Second, if you wake up in the morning and do not want to get out of bed, then you are probably pursuing the wrong goals for you. Don't get me wrong; I was very proud of what we had accomplished in opening the restaurants. Specifically, actually opening ten BKs in ten consecutive weeks, but after that, my life became about doing the activities necessary to maintain the business—not as good a fit for me, personally.

I realized I prefer a corporate environment so I accepted an area coach position with Jack in the Box in Washington state. The following year, I was promoted to region vice president for Los Angeles. In accepting this promotion, I found I had to learn many new skills. My career prior to Los Angeles had been based on taking newly-hired or poor performance stores and raising the execution levels. Now, I was assuming responsibility for one of the best company-operated regions in the company. The goal became not just executing at the highest levels but also developing the team to ensure we could replicate our performance within other parts of the company. These successes led to my promotion as a region group vice president operating three western Jack in the Box regions.

We all have setbacks of one type or another in our careers; mine was the elimination of my position in 2010. At first, like many people during that time, I was devastated, but after a few months, I realized I had been given a gift. Not necessarily an "Oh great, here is a surprise," but rather an opportunity to decide what I really wanted to do with the rest of my life. We get into a career, and often, we let the path we are going down just dictate where we are going. At least, I knew I had been doing just that. I enjoyed my previous life, but I had stopped asking myself whether this was what I really wanted to do. So I did just that! In the next several months, I read at least four books, hired a coach, and I tried introspection. What did I find? Well, I found what I missed. I missed networking, leading people, and taking on challenges we all face in our work lives. In the end, I took two years just to enjoy myself and figure out what I wanted to do. I volunteered with Big Brothers, Big Sisters in Los Angeles as chair of the board, focusing on our service and financial strength, so we as an agency could increase the number of children we serve each year. (In 2012, I was awarded "National Board Member of the Year.) I also returned to my career, a company that truly aligns with my own career goals, a company that believes in servant leadership, taking care of and developing its people, and where the culture can truly represent the organization's success. Today, I am much more enthusiastic, excited to get up in the morning, and looking forward to creating new successes as a Zone Leader at 7-Eleven in Northern California/Nevada.

Nina: As you look back over your career, what is the one thing you've learned that you would like to share with other women?

Nancy: First, communicate honestly; by that, I mean that we frequently try to couch our messages in a "nice, don't hurt anyone's feelings" kind of way. I am not saying to be rude or even overly blunt, but to be successful, you must not avoid a potential conflict because it is a tough conversation.

Second, you must find excitement (or fun) within your job/ career. No one likes every aspect of her job, but if you cannot get excited about your job every day, how can anyone else?

Nina: If you could do one thing over in your business career, what would it be?

Nancy: I would have asked myself what I really wanted to do with my career more frequently and honestly.

Nina: Why do you feel you are so successful?

Nancy: When I am truly successful, I have taken the time to define my purpose; I have built an excitement about it within myself. This then spreads to those around me. We can create a common vision about our path and we are all the better for it.

Nina: How much time do you spend networking?

Nancy: Never as much as I should. Unfortunately, most of us do not place a high enough value on networking whether it is through new connections or revitalizing current and older relationships.

Nina: For a female who is either starting or rejoining the business world, what advice would you give her?

Nancy: Learn as much as you can about your current pursuits. Ask questions—if you are ever afraid to ask questions, it may not be an environment in which you want to stay or at least an environment you want to work at changing.

Nina: What has been your greatest obstacle in your career?

Nancy: Getting so focused on achieving my end goal that I have missed great things along the way.

Nina: How did you overcome that obstacle?

Nancy: I started listening more and realized that as a leader, my real job is to develop others in the process because we will all be more effective.

Nina: Given a platform to speak to women, is there anything else you would like to say to them?

Nancy: We have to be confident in who we are, even if that confidence is rooted in "I don't really know who or what I am right now, but I am trying to find my way and that is all right." I realize that may sound trite, but there will be times you may find you are less accepted because you are a woman, but there are times a man is less accepted as well. There are times we are all frustrated and feel we deserve more, but even those times help to create who we are along the way.

Interview #8

JAMIE EDEN

Area Director for Del Taco Corporate

Nina: Thank you, Jamie, for agreeing to this interview. What is your current position?

Jamie: Area Director for Del Taco.

Nina: How did you get started in your career? And why did you pick the restaurant industry?

Jamie: In 1997, I began my career in the food industry as a cashier for Burger King. I applied there after my separation of fifteen years of marriage. I was a housewife and lived my younger years as a mother and wife who supported her family emotionally. At the time of the divorce, reality set in that I was a single parent with no experience as well as no work history. I had found myself head of the house hold with no real education or employable assets.

When I began working as a cashier, I was thirty-two years of age working with teenagers who were faster on their feet and quicker at learning. Even though my self-esteem was low and I was very discouraged, I did not let that stop me. I showed up to work every day on time and gave it 100 percent. After a year, a new general manager came in who saw something in me that I did not even see in myself; she gave me an opportunity to learn a management position. I worked hard and studied till I couldn't see straight. I worked any shift given to me and took any advice people would give me. After working for a year or so as a shift leader, I was then promoted to an assistant general manager position. This is where I learned the skills of running restaurant operations. About six months later, my general manager got sick and my district manager asked whether he should bring someone in to run the store or whether I thought I could do it. I can remember taking a deep breath, and with every ounce of courage I had, I said, "YES." I wanted to give it try. And I did. I worked just as hard as I could and just kept moving forward no matter what I might have felt inside. I can even remember people telling me along the way that I couldn't do it. People who were close to me. I tried to block out the negative and just pushed forward through all my fears and doubts. And I did it.

I became a very successful general manager who was passionate about the business and just really wanted to succeed. I knew at this point that I could do anything I put my mind to. My two girls also motivated me throughout this time and told me, "Mom, you can do it; we believe in you." It was hard, but not impossible. From there, I was promoted to a training manager and developed many shift leaders as well as future general managers. I was a great trainer because of where I had started. The scared, insecure, single mother helped me not to give up on anyone who was willing and motivated. I shared any and all knowledge I had received through my own life experiences and my team responded. From there, I became a district manager for Burger King. Wow, that again was another eye-opener. All of my fears and doubts emerged once again, but again, I said, "Yes" to the position and a journey began of managing without any control. In my restaurant, I had full control, but as a district manager, you have none. You must get your job done through others.

This position was a struggle for me because of my past. It is very hard to release control when all you have to control is your life. I struggled as a new district manager and was transferred to being a director of training. As a director of training, I learned many skills. I learned that we were really in the people business. And I could not succeed myself unless others succeeded. I learned how to motivate and encourage people to be whomever and whatever they wanted to be. I became their self-confidence until they found theirs like I once did.

After two years of training, I tried the district manager position again, and with the tools I had learned along the way, I became successful. Then another opportunity came around—director of operations. I was going to manage the whole company. Oh my God…could I do it? Could I make the impact through other district managers and lead a company? Well, again I said, "Yes" and gave it a whirl. I did this for several years and really learned what professionalism was. I again had great people who took me under their wings and taught me the corporate life and how to survive. Nina, you were one of those people. You taught me what professionalism was and never to let them see you sweat. From you

I learned how to keep my composure at all times because when you get too passionate about things, people stop listening to you. You taught me how to survive in "a man's world." This was by far my hardest lesson that I learned.

Nina: As you look back over your career, what is the one thing you learned that you would like to share with other women?

Jamie: Don't let your emotions get in the way. Keep those thoughts inside. Yes, they could be right, and yes, you feel them for good reason, but people stop listening if you allow your emotions to come out. I can remember crying in front of my peers (mostly male peers) and they looked at me like I was crazy. So the one thing I can share is that, yes, you can be passionate and love what you do, but the delivery of the message is how you make the changes. Some wars you win; some you lose, but now I choose the ones I want to fight, and the ones that give the biggest impact.

Nina: If you could do one thing over in your business career, what would that be?

Jamie: Attend school and get a degree. It is so hard to fit it in later rather than earlier. I have still not given up on this one though!

Nina: Why do you feel you are successful?

Jamie: I feel successful because I have not allowed anyone to keep me from trying. I have potential. All the things that were told to me from such a small age as a girl have not stopped me. People who knew me back when I was a teenager never thought that Jamie would succeed. But guess what? I have. My close friends and my young adult girls have seen where I came from and where I am at now. I feel blessed that I have had people in my life to teach me what success looks and feels like.

Nina: How much time do you spend networking?

Jamie: I network every day. I stay in contact with professional people and surround myself with those who are ambitious and want to do better.

Nina: For a female who is either starting or rejoining the business world, what advice would you give her?

Jamie: Don't ever give up on yourself. You make your own destiny. Don't sell yourself short.

Nina: What has been your greatest obstacle in your career?

Jamie: My greatest obstacle in my career I would have to say is managing my feelings. It's just business.

Nina: How did you overcome that obstacle?

Jamie: Okay, here is my trick. When I start to feel the "passion/emotion" coming out, I start to breathe. I begin to speak slower, and this truly does relax my feeling and thoughts. I can then communicate in a calm, cool, and collected manner.

Nina: Given the platform to speak to women, is there anything else you would like to say to them?

Jamie: We are smart. We are intelligent, and we can do anything we put our minds too. We can have it all. We can be successful *and* be good moms, wives, sisters, and daughters.

Interview #9

TRACY KEARNS

National Account Executive with
Dr. Pepper Snapple Group

Nina: Thank you, Tracy, for agreeing to be interviewed. What is your current position?

Tracy: National Account Executive with Dr. Pepper Snapple Group. (Initially, I was hired by Dr. Pepper/Seven Up; the company became Cadbury Schweppes Americas Beverages, and is now DPSG.)

Nina: Can you give me the details about your career from its beginning until now?

Tracy: I attended Cal Poly Pomona from '93 to '97 at a later age than traditional students. After a series of administrative positions, I redirected my career path to sales. I started with Dr. Pepper in 1997 as an associate account sales manager and began to learn about the soft drink business (as well as the food service industry). I moved from a territorial associate to account sales manager, and eventually, I moved to our national accounts team as part of the Burger Team in 2000. I made a lateral move to our corporate office in 2004 as a sales planning manager. I returned to our Burger King field team in 2006 in the national associate executive position.

Nina: As you look back over your career, what is the one thing you learned that you would like to share with other women?

Tracy: I believe finding mentors (both internally and externally) is essential for career growth and guidance. Initially, I was unaware of this—and only realized the value of mentors over time.

Nina: If you could do one thing over in your business career, what would it be?

Tracy: I would have started sooner. I truly did not focus on my career until my early thirties.

Nina: Why do you feel you are so successful?

Tracy: I have a strong interest in developing and fostering relationships. The ability to leverage this passion has allowed me to gain confidence and grow in my position.

Nina: How much time do you spend networking?

Tracy: I spend approximately 5-8 hours per week networking (primarily informally) split between face-to-face and e-mail/phone conversations.

Nina: For a female who is either starting or rejoining the business world, what advice would you give her?

Tracy: I would advise her to seek out mentors and career advocates early on!

Nina: What has been your greatest obstacle in your career?

Tracy: Probably fear and lack of confidence.

Nina: How did you overcome that obstacle?

Tracy: Over time...becoming more adept at recognizing when my own thoughts and doubts are hindering action. Being exposed to strong women over time has helped me recognize and minimize my fears.

Nina: Given a platform to speak to women, is there anything else you would like to say to them?

Tracy: I would say to keep an open mind, and don't be shy to ask successful people to share their insights. Make networking a priority and find enjoyment in what you do.

Interview #10

JUDY HOFF

Executive Director of Queen, It's a New Day

Nina: Thank you, Judy, for agreeing to do this interview. What is your current position?

Judy: My current position is Executive Director of Queen, It's a New Day, a nonprofit organization. I am the author of a book called *Healing the Hole In Your Heart: Transform Your Devastation into Empowerment and Create the Life of Your Dreams*. I am also a speaker and a professional pastoral counselor.

Nina: How did you come to the decision that you wanted this career?

Judy: My current career is part of a journey over many years that started with knowing I am a natural people helper. I started my career as a medical hypnotherapist. I was trained by the man who started the school and mentored into this field of the mind-body connection. I specialized in pain management and created products that were used in hospitals for arthritis and cancer sufferers to aid them in natural pain relief, as well as stress management, habit control, and sports improvement products. I was a speaker at colleges and hospitals too.

Then I went back to school and received an A.A. degree in human services and onward I went into the chemical dependency profession and worked at a in-patient program, then ran an outpatient program. I worked with at risk people for the city as a prevention program developer. Onward again to Bible college. I earned a B.A. in ministry leadership. Then I served and started many outreach programs for the community such as Queen, It's a New Day, Life Support, and Biblical Counseling, training the community, along with starting a large department for counselors.

This theme of always growing is part of me; I never stay in one job; I just keep moving forward, which requires change! Next stop, a huge ministry, called Life Changes, with housing programs for men, women, and children in transition, including being the pastor of the church. Today, I am enjoying developing a speaking career, along with operating Queen, It's a New Day. My hope is to reach many communities, transforming communities one woman at a time.

Nina: As you look back over your career, what is the one thing you have learned that you would like to share with other women?

Judy: As I look back, I have learned always to be ready for change and growth. Life is interesting, and new opportunities await those who will embrace change!

Nina: Why do you feel you are successful?

Judy: I give my success over to the giver of gifts, Jesus Christ. He has equipped me to do all things through Him who strengthens me!

Nina: How much time do you spend networking?

Judy: My life is a network! Building relationships with people is part of God's plan. Love God, love yourself, and love others.

Nina: For a female who is either starting or rejoining the business world, what advice would you give her?

Judy: Be yourself! Let your gifts shine, and do not compare yourself to others.

Nina: What has been your greatest obstacle in your career?

Judy: I think my opinion of my own self-worth has been my greatest obstacle.

Nina: How did you overcome that obstacle?

Judy: I am still overcoming my false self-belief system. When I doubt myself, I remember who my daddy is—God! I tell myself what He says about me, and every day I get more confident.

Nina: Given a platform to speak to women, is there anything else you would like to say to them?

Judy: Women, be what God made you to be, and keep your eyes on Him. Forgive others and yourself. The past is finished so look forward. Keep your eyes on your goals and visualize what you want to experience, the life of your dreams!

Interview #11

REBECCA CLARK

General Manager in Senior Housing

Nina: Thank you, Rebecca, for agreeing to this interview. What is your current position?

Rebecca: I am currently general manager of a large independent and assisted living community (senior housing) in Woodinville. I have been here seventeen years...hard to believe but true!

Nina: How did you decide on this career?

Rebecca: I transitioned to this career from the private club industry. I was employed by Club Corporation of America for fifteen years, in a variety of roles. Club Corp was a privately owned company specializing in private country clubs, tennis and athletic clubs, and resorts and "city" clubs, for example, Columbia Tower Club in Seattle. In my years with Club Corp, I was involved in sales and marketing at the club level, the regional sales and marketing director (the West Coast and Hawaii!), general manager, and moved to feasibility studies and development.

When we divested a property I was working at in Bellevue, I chose not to remain in the field. I travelled extensively and was working most nights and weekends. It was not conducive to a lifestyle that I wanted for myself, and it was not conducive to family life. It was sexy, though!

As we divested the club, I was invited (by a board member) to consider working in the senior housing industry. I felt it would be a solid career, given the target market, and it would be conducive to my lifestyle. By that time, I had a nine-year-old daughter, and I felt I needed to be front and center in her life. My current position allowed me the freedom and flexibility to manage (for the most part) my own time, and it is located only one mile from my home. I felt like I was a "stay at home mom"—with a job. I work for a company that allows me to put my family first and that is the most important thing to me. Over the years, I have given up many advancement opportunities due to my commitment to child raising. That is not a decision I regret, and I would do the same again.

Prior to my "corporate careers," I worked as a surveyor on the Alaska Pipeline, taught skiing in Colorado, and owned a commercial fishing boat in Alaska. It was a good life—lots of fun and interesting.

Bottom line, I did not originally want to be in this current career, but it has suited my personal needs.

Nina: As you look back over your career, what is the one thing you learned that you would like to share with other women?

Rebecca: That we are good business people, good people managers, and we are very, very capable. We cannot, however, "have it all," without someone paying the price.

Nina: If you could do one thing over in your business career, what would it be?

Rebecca: Get a college degree; I don't have one and it has held me back because I thought no one would hire me. Maybe true; maybe not. But, I do believe other doors would have been opened to me if I had one. Also, have more confidence in myself, my earning capacity, and my own intelligence. Not sell myself short.

Nina: Why do you feel you are so successful?

Rebecca: I am successful because of the people who work for me and with me. I can only be as good as the weakest link on the team. I am a good judge of people; I seem to be able to lead them, and they want to "please" me. I believe I create a good place for people to work, to grow, and to feel proud of their accomplishments. I recognize talent and am able to nurture talent in people and move them on their way. I am also honest and direct. No game playing. People appear to appreciate that trait.

Nina: How much time do you spend networking?

Rebecca: Not that much; I should do more. I'm just not motivated in that way...I'm good at "connecting the dots," but I'm not one for organized networking meetings.

Nina: For a female who is either starting or rejoining the business world, what advice would you give her?

Rebecca: Have confidence in yourself. Many, many of the skills you have utilized in the home and/or raising children are the same skills that are appropriate in the workplace.

Nina: What has been your greatest obstacle in your career?

Rebecca: Myself.

Nina: How did you overcome that obstacle?

Rebecca: I'm not sure I have.

Nina: Given a platform to speak to women, is there anything else you would like to say to them?

Rebecca: Oh, lots of things I would love to say...have confidence, know you're worth it, don't sell yourself short, don't take less money than you're worth, don't put up with any garbage—move on or move out. Be nice. Handle "power" with grace. Be honest. Be kind. Above all, have a sense of humor. Don't whine; don't play games. Keep yourself well-groomed; go for class; don't exploit your femininity.

Interview #12

DENISE JACKSON

Distributor Beverage Manager for PepsiCo

Nina: Thank you, Denise, for agreeing to this interview. What is your current position?

Denise: Distributor Beverage Manager—Washington, Oregon, and Alaska for PepsiCo.

Nina: How did you come to the decision that you wanted a career in consumer products?

Denise: Once I graduated from college, I began my career at Procter & Gamble. I was very fortunate to have great mentors and was allowed to touch all sides of the consumer products business. Working for P&G allowed me to expand my skill sets and learn how to become a great leader.

Nina: Can you give me some detail about your career from its beginning until now?

Denise: At P&G I held multiple roles, including key account manager, category management analyst, wholesale channel category manager, and retail key account manager, to name just a few. After sixteen years and surviving six restructures, my role had been relocated to another state. With the offer on the table and no option to stay in Seattle, I declined the position and left P&G. The main driver behind this decision was my children. No amount of money could replace the network of friends who were available if I needed any assistance, and I did not want to relocate my family. Change is difficult, and after so much time with one organization, it was almost like experiencing a loss. I went to work immediately after for a couple of years for Nestle, which was based in Seattle, until I started working with PepsiCo. The opportunity to work with PepsiCo on its food service team was the last sector of the business where I needed to gain experience in all channels of the consumer product portfolio. I have been very fortunate to work for firms that are in the Top 100 Fortune 500 organizations and have set myself up to lead a team.

Nina: As you look back over your career, what is the one thing you learned that you would like to share with other women?

Denise: My first priority was and will always be my kids. I chose my career path with opportunities that allowed me to be home-based with minimal travel to raise my family. As a single mom, the choices I made to be with them resulted in a career path that made it challenging financially. Looking back, I would not change one moment or my decision because my children are now almost grown and will be able to have their own careers. I have set myself up for success by committing to learn all the facets of the business, and now that my family responsibilities are changing, I am in a position to begin to escalate my career. I can look back on all these years and count on one hand the number of events I have missed for my kids, but for the rest, I was always there. I am so thankful for my family and my life, and I am excited for the next phase of my journey.

Nina: Why do you feel you are so successful?

Denise: I believe I am successful because I have never ever given up on anything. Over the years, many people have asked me how I survive and manage my family on my own. What I tell them is, “You do what you know,” and for me, it is the norm. I strive every day to be positive and be a great role model for my children. Nothing is impossible if you just believe!

Nina: How much time do you spend networking?

Denise: Networking is critical to finding your path, and I have begun to network, but not nearly enough. My goal is to reach out once a week, but I continue to place it within the parameters of my week on my business plan.

Nina: For a female who is either starting in or rejoining the business world, what advice would you give her?

Denise: Spend some time understanding and getting clarity on exactly what you are looking for, and be very clear on what things are non-negotiable situations for you and your family. Be brave enough to look at the possibility of failure or potential obstacles, and really celebrate your successes, no matter how small.

Nina: What has been your greatest obstacle in your career?

Denise: I'm not sure that I have had a greatest obstacle. I just tackle them as they come and work through them. I believe that I can do anything and can survive anything.

Nina: Given a platform to speak to women, is there anything else you would like to say to them?

Denise: Trust and believe in yourself because it starts within you. It is so easy to compromise and give up what you are truly passionate about because it is less difficult. You will be challenged every day, but welcome the challenge as a learning experience for the journey to your goal. Strive to have a work-life balance, and remember, you cannot bring back the moments you missed, so make sure you choose wisely. BELIEVE.

Interview #13

CAROL LEE

Founder of TruePax

Nina: Thank you, Carol, for agreeing to this interview. What is your current position?

Carol: TruePax founder, community concierge, coach, and connector.

Nina: Can you give me some detail about your career from beginning until now? And how did you come to the decision that you wanted to be in this career?

Carol: I had an interest in fashion merchandising and started an internship when I was fifteen, working in a high-end retail shop while in high school. I loved it! From that point on, I knew it was a field I could excel in, so I focused all my work experiences and educational choices in that area.

Nina: As you look back over your career, what is the one thing you learned that you would like to share with other women?

Carol: Find your passion, do something you love, and aim high! Be open to new experiences and view the world as a learning ground. There are no limits when you are operating in your true calling!

Nina: If you could do one thing over in your business career, what would that be?

Carol: Start my second career earlier! It is wonderful to be using my gifts and talents this time around.

Nina: Why do you feel you are so successful?

Carol: I am blessed with family, love, friends, health, and a calling. As I realize what the Lord has given me, it is astounding. Success is wanting what you have and I am so thankful.

Nina: How much time do you spend networking?

Carol: Daily, as I go through my everyday activities. If you have an open spirit and take an interest in people, it becomes part of who you are. Networking is discovering people's unique stories and callings, and then using connections for win-win outcomes. When you have a heart to help build relationships and community, you will draw like-minded people.

Nina: For a female who is either starting in or rejoining the business world, what advice would you give her?

Carol: Tap into your God-given talents, do some soul-searching, and reach deep. Discover what ignites you, and pursue opportunities that align with your passion. Reach out and meet others; we all need others to join us on our journey. Make a difference; live a life that inspires others.

Nina: What has been your greatest obstacle in your career?

Carol: Not enough hours in the day and other responsibilities that take priority. Achieving balance is a lifelong challenge as priorities change and seasons evolve. It is important to keep focused on what really matters and keep that on the top of your "To Do" list.

Nina: How did you overcome that obstacle?

Carol: By being patient and realizing that there is a season for everything. Also, by remembering that being true to who you are and your unique calling is a life well-lived.

Nina: Given a platform to speak to women, is there anything else you would like to say to them?

Carol: Be true to yourself. Be fearless in your pursuit of a life lived well. Treat others with respect and honor their unique gifts. Hold onto your dreams and never hesitate to dream big. Use your gifts to impact the world and make a difference. Leave a legacy. Live a life of no regrets. Love God and love others. Surround yourself with others who are positive and like-minded and spirited, and limit exposure to those who bring you down and drain you. Life is too short to waste your emotional energy. After all, there is so much to accomplish!

Interview #14

CINDY COUYOUMJIAN

Principal for Cinergy Financial

Nina: Thanks, Cindy, for agreeing to this interview. What is your current position?

Cindy: I am a certified financial planner and a principal for my office that manages four registered representatives and works with individuals in navigating their financial goals.

Nina: How did you decide this is the career you wanted? Can you give me some detail about your career from its beginning until now?

Cindy: I started in the business in 1986. I graduated from college with a marketing degree. My desire was to be in sales, and I had an interest in being a stockbroker. I was referred to a friend who worked for Equitable. I was granted an interview. I was hired and worked eighteen years for the firm. I went back to college and received my CFP in 1991.

Nina: As you look back over your career, what is the one thing you learned that you would like to share with other women?

Cindy: To be successful, you need to be driven. Setting goals has been my number one driver. No goals! No accomplishments! I set annual goals and execute them rather than just talk about them. Also, you have to be honest, have integrity, and have perseverance to get through obstacles. It's almost like being in denial when problems arise. You have to get rid of all your bad habits, choose healthy lifestyle choices, and get rid of distractions that will keep you from being focused. I call it *hypo-focused*—keeping your eye on the prize. Problems and issues will arise in your career; being able to shake things off quickly and stay focused on your goals is what it is all about. Be willing to do things others don't want to do.

Nina: If you could do one thing over in your business career, what would that be?

Cindy: Find a mentor or coach to help me work smarter. Keeping the learning curve at a minimum. Spending more time networking. Finding someone to motivate me.

Nina: Why do you feel you are successful?

Cindy: Feeling successful has to do with making a difference, being happy, and being driven to serve others based on *love!*

Nina: How much time do you spend networking?

Cindy: I don't spend much time networking, and that has hindered me.

Nina: For a female who is either starting or rejoining the business world, what advice would you give her?

Cindy: Become an expert in what you do. Know more than others, and have others help you grow your business. Have love and passion in everything you do. Be professional, but the new paradigm shift has to do with being *personal!* Get to know people as you would a new friend!

Nina: What has been your greatest obstacle in your career?

Cindy: Putting in the time to get the experience to be the best at what you do!

Nina: How did you overcome that obstacle?

Cindy: I overcome obstacles by forgetting the problem and persevering forward. "Denial" is the best word I can find to overcome obstacles.

Nina: Given a platform to speak to women, is there anything else you would like to say to them?

Cindy: Women have a huge advantage in business—the emotional nature we have as beings—and, of course, our multi-tasking God-given ability. Use those gifts to the fullest. However, we lack confidence, and that can defeat us by making us feel as if we are a minority in business. You have to change that thought process. Dress for success. Fake it till you make it!

Last, but not least, it is important to have a faith walk to get you through your darkest moments in your personal and business life. Without it, I would have never been successful. God needs to be on your team to succeed. Life is challenging, and work is part of it. Think of trials as opportunities to learn. Look at the good and positive in everything negative. Tithing 10 percent of my income has also been a critical aspect of my success—probably, as I look back, the most important! Giving back is a way of being thankful for all the blessings in life. The more you give, the more you get. You can never out-give God. He blesses abundantly and provides you everything you need. If people take the time to analyze the results, they will be amazed. Tithing is something I started in 2000, and I will never stop. Money has so many temptations with it, no matter what disciplines in life you came from concerning money. You want something to help you manage that evil in the world. Tithing is the key, no matter how little or how great your earning power is. It is hard to do but very gratifying. This discipline and philosophy protects you from the evils of the world, and it provides you more than you ever imagined!

Interview #15

TANA BAUMLER

Restaurant Owner and Operator

Nina: Thank you, Tana, for agreeing to this interview. What is your current position?

Tana: Restaurant owner, manager, and operator.

Nina: Can you give me some details about your career from its beginning until now? And how did you come to the decision you wanted to be in this career?

Tana: My family owned a pie baking business, and I have been in the restaurant industry most of my life. I have traveled through Europe, experimenting with different spices and foods, learning to use different cooking techniques. I have always had an interest in food so opening a restaurant felt like second nature.

Nina: As you look back over your career, what is the one thing you learned that you would like to share with other women?

Tana: First, listen to other people's advice, but always go with your gut feeling! Second, when an issue comes up, resolve it as soon as possible. Sometimes we are too busy to take care of issues, and then the small things become large things later on.

Nina: If you could do one thing over in your business career, what would that be?

Tana: Nothing. I think failures teach you as much as success does.

Nina: Why do you feel you are so successful?

Tana: I believe I have the right combination of service, food, and atmosphere. You are only as good as your employees, and I have fabulous employees. Another reason is I am here and work my business. You can't hire people to run your business; you have to be invested and take the time to work the floor with your employees.

Nina: How much time do you spend networking?

Tana: Always. No matter where I am, I am talking to people about my business. It always seems to be coming up.

Nina: For a female who is either starting or rejoining the business world, what advice would you give her?

Tana: Go work for someone in the field you want to open your business in. Do your homework.

Nina: What has been your greatest obstacle in your career?

Tana: Trying to juggle family, friends, and other interests while trying to run a successful business.

Nina: How did you overcome that obstacle?

Tana: Surrounding myself with good, supportive people.

Nina: Given a platform to speak to women, is there anything else you would like to say to them?

Tana: Don't forget the people closest to you; they are your support system. Do not be afraid to ask questions and advice from people in your related industry.

Interview #16

ELIZABETH TOBIAS

Marketing Manager with a Global Fast Food Chain

Nina: Thank you, Elizabeth, for agreeing to do this interview. What is your current position?

Elizabeth: Marketing manager with a global fast food chain.

Nina: How did you come to the decision that you wanted a career in marketing? Can you give me some details about your career from its beginning until now?

Elizabeth: When I started college, I had no idea what I wanted to major in. I eventually had to declare a major, so I decided on business because it was so broad. Once I was in business school, I met with an advisor who asked what kind of job I wanted when I graduated. I didn't have a specific position in mind, so I just described what I wanted to do. I recall indicating that I wanted to be a company representative who went out and met with people and talked about the company's products. The advisor did the best he could with my limited information and suggested I go into marketing.

I moved to England while in my twenties and found a great entry level marketing position through a temporary agency.

It was supposed to be an eight-week assignment, but I was asked to join the company after they saw that I could do the job well and that I was a hard worker. I stayed there for two-and-a-half years.

When I moved back to the States, I found another job through a temp agency: this was with a small advertising agency, and again, I was able to prove myself quickly and got hired full-time. I advanced during my eight years at the agency; then the agency lost its main client and the agency went from a staff of fifty-five to nine, and I was one of the nine. I think I was kept on because I was a smart and hard worker, but also I think I was a great value to the company. (I wasn't a great negotiator when it came to salary.)

At the end of my time with this small agency, I started work on an MBA as a part-time student in the evenings. I did this because I wanted something challenging and new in my life and I have always loved learning. I found a new job with a top-tier ad agency working on a global brand and absolutely loved it. I finished the MBA program after four years and finally felt like I had made it. After three years on the account, I transferred from the St. Louis to the L.A. office, still on the same account. The client then went through a succession of agency changes, and each time, they asked that I be brought along. I had substantial pay increases over the years, but I maintained an account supervisor title the entire ten years with the agencies. I enjoyed the job and didn't feel the need or drive to do something else. The client asked me to join their in-house marketing team: they had seen me work, and I knew I was a great fit. I've had that position for six years. I haven't had to interview for most of the jobs I have had;

my skills and work ethic were noted by those I worked with, and each time, that led to the next opportunity.

Nina: As you look back over your career, what is the one thing you learned that you would like to share with other women?

Elizabeth: Don't wait for things to happen to you; make them happen. Get involved: attend office get-togethers, join the company's co-ed softball team, take the lead in volunteer activities. Maintain a positive attitude; it's a very attractive quality.

Nina: If you could do one thing over in your business career, what would that be?

Elizabeth: Well, there are lots of things I would have done differently, but most importantly, I would have found a mentor or two along the way. Mentoring was not a concept that I had even heard about or considered when I was starting my career, and looking back, I think I could have gone so much further if I had found someone to provide a little guidance and push.

Nina: Why do you feel you are so successful?

Elizabeth: I think work ethic has a lot to do with my success. People want me on their team, and clients respect me because they know I will work hard for them. I listen, and because of this, I gain an understanding of what is important to people; this has been a huge help in the sales part of my job. I'm professional in the way I act and present myself.

Nina: How much time do you spend networking?

Elizabeth: It's only recently that I started doing a good job of networking, and now I see the power in it. I aim to reach out to or meet with a couple of people every week; I attend work-related conferences and seminars whenever possible, and I also am involved in volunteer activities and have made some fantastic contacts that way. So in terms of time spent networking, each week it can range from just a half-hour of phone calls or emails to an hour having coffee with a business associate, or several hours at a seminar or happy hour meeting new people. There are just so many ways to network!

Nina: For a female who is either starting in or rejoining the business world, what advice would you give her?

Elizabeth: Think about what you really want to do and be able to articulate it quickly and clearly. Networking is key. People love to help, so don't be afraid to ask. Make sure the culture of the company is a good fit for you.

Nina: What has been your greatest obstacle in your career?

Elizabeth: Lack of knowledge—not knowing what I didn't know. This is where a mentor or better networking earlier in my career would have been a huge help.

Nina: How did you overcome that obstacle?

Elizabeth: Even though I am more than two-thirds of the way through my career, it's never too late to learn. I now seek out peoples' opinions and advice, and I am always looking to expand my business network.

Nina: Given a platform to speak to women, is there anything else you would like to say to them?

Elizabeth: Be confident and maintain a positive outlook. Stay away from the petty stuff that naturally comes up in any workplace. Don't be intimidated by others. Do your best to prepare.

Interview #17

FRITZI WOODS

President and CEO of the Women's Food Service Forum (WFF)

Nina: Thank you, Fritzi, for taking the time to share your knowledge with women. What is your current position?

Fritzi: President and CEO of the Women's Food Service Forum.

Nina: If there is one thing you would like to tell women about business, what would that be?

Fritzi: Make sure you truly understand how the company you are working for makes money; truly learn how the operations/company functions.

Nina: Looking back at your career, what is the best decision you made?

Fritzi: Continually getting out of my comfort zone, taking risks to learn and potentially fail, and letting that fear drive me to do my best.

Nina: Along those lines, is there any one decision you made that if you could go back you would do differently?

Fritzi: I wish there was only one. I would continually build strategic networks at every step in my career. There is a theme—asking for help sooner when things were not working.

Nina: What do you think is the biggest mistake we make in business?

Fritzi: We do not do enough due diligence about the opportunities we get. My experience is that we tend to get offered the really, really tough assignments. That's okay, but we just need to understand that, and then *ask for resources* so we can be successful without killing ourselves.

Nina: I have emphasized in my book how important networking is in business. The WFF is one of the best networking organizations for women. Will you tell us in your words what is the best benefit WFF offers and how each woman can join this organization?

Fritzi:

1. Strategic networks, commonly framed as sponsors most recently in most studies, are absolutely critical for women to advance in their careers. Networking is critical at all stages of your career. These sponsors, advocates, mentors (your strategic network) not only represent you when you are not in the room, but they are critical in your career progression to ensure you are getting the right jobs (content/experience). You can be brilliant and not get the right opportunities. Networks are a must have. WFF creates multiple platforms for

you to build strategic networks. To build relationships that matter in your career.

2. Relevant content—leadership competency-based critical skills and behaviors that you need. We have an online assessment tool to help you understand your gaps with input from others.
3. www.WomensFoodServiceForum.com. Join online—membership is $199 per year with great benefits. Or contact Karen Lazowski: klazowski@wff.org

Interview #18

MARIA COASSIN

Founder and Owner of Gelatiamo

Nina: Thank you, Maria, for agreeing to do this interview. What is your current position?

Maria: I am the founder and owner of Gelatiamo, Seattle's most famous gelateria and pastry shop.

Nina: Can you give me some detail about your career from its beginning until now? And how did you come to the decision that you wanted to be in this career?

Maria: I grew up in a family of bakers in Northern Italy. My family has owned and operated bakeries for over two hundred years. I can say that the business was in my DNA, although I took it in a little different direction, moving from breads to making gelato. I always worked in my family business, and when I got married, I moved to the United States. Under my father's suggestion twenty-five years ago, before I even moved here, I started to think about what I could do when I moved. The thought of being a baker wasn't too appealing to me because of the early working hours, but the idea of having my own business was something that was kind of expected of me (according to my father) since that is all I knew at that point in my life (and according to my father, I had what it took to give it a try).

The region I grew up in has had a very long string of gelato makers who have moved around the world, opening up very successful businesses, so with many of my own friends having such businesses, I decided to investigate the possibility of getting started.

I became familiar with all that it took to start a gelato business before I even left Italy, and when in early January 1992, I moved to California, my real journey began. I didn't speak English, aside from what little I had learned in school, and that wasn't even enough to get me a sales associate position, let alone a job that would even remotely compare to what I had in Italy.

My first job here was at McDonald's. I was hired on to take care of the lobby and the restroom facilities...that didn't last long because after just a few days, I was moved to the kitchen, and from there, I rose to a supervisory position in very little time, despite the fact that my language skills weren't excellent. I treasure that experience more than anyone will ever know because it taught me so much in terms of how to run a successful food operation and, with the idea of opening my own food business, that was a priceless experience for me. It was my first working experience outside the family business. It taught me how to create a structured environment, the importance of training manuals, store policies, how to deal with employees, and it exposed me to real business practices in this country. I have learned a great deal from working in such an amazing organization, and even if you might not like it, you still need to admire the success that McDonald's has all over the world.

After eighteen months, I moved to Seattle, and it was then that the planning of Gelatiamo began. I still needed to improve my language skills before I could open my business, and I also needed more managerial experience. So, for the next few years, I worked as a manager for a local educational supplier company. Doing that gave me the opportunity to improve my English and become more aware of America's history and culture, along with gaining additional managerial skills because there I was dealing with buyers, institutions, parents, kids, and professionals.

While I was working, I started to take trips back to Italy to learn about recipe development and acquire more in-depth knowledge about the gelato business. After a couple of years of back and forth, I was offered a very high position within the company as a regional manager. It was at that point that I felt that if someone had that much confidence in my managerial abilities, it meant I was ready to put all that I had learned into action, and strong in my gelato knowledge, I started looking at possible locations.

It wasn't an easy process. Commercial real estate was at its peak; few locations were available, and they were very expensive; interest rates were out of this world. But I put together a business plan, started looking at financing, despite the fact that I was (with my father's help) investing a substantial amount of money. Committed as I was to making my dream come true, I found a location right in downtown Seattle. It had everything one would want: southwest exposure, a corner location, lots of windows, the possibility for an outside patio, and lots of foot traffic. It wasn't until I signed the lease and started construction that I realized it wasn't as perfect as I had thought, but that wasn't even the only mistake I made….

It was a hard beginning, but I had put everything I had into it, and it was what I had set out to do, so I kept going. I had many ups and down; I had to make many financial, personal, and emotional sacrifices, but in the end, it was all worth it. My career has now taken a new path. Not only am I a successful business owner, but I also have an opportunity to teach and inspire others who want to get into my industry.

Nina: As you look back over your career, what is the one thing you learned that you would like to share with other women?

Maria: Don't give up. Keep your dream alive and fight for it. Women make amazing business owners. Our attention to detail, our organizational skills, and our ability to be passionate about what we do are characteristics that are not often found in men but natural in women. The business world is still a male-dominated one, and as women, we always pay a higher price to be entrepreneurs, but when we get there, we are much more likely to stay because we fight harder to keep going.

Nina: If you could do one thing over in your business career, what would that be?

Maria: I wouldn't change a thing. With today's knowledge, I would make different business decisions, and that is because of experience, but I wouldn't change the path that took me to where I am today. I feel that I am a much better woman today than I would have been if I had never walked down this road.

Nina: Why do you feel you are so successful?

Maria: I think it is the passion that I infused into my business and my willingness not to compromise. Success doesn't just happen; it takes a lot of hard work and commitment. Failure wasn't an option for me, and I did all I could to make my dream come true. Quality, tradition, and passion. Excellent quality products, knowledge, and expertise, passion for what I do that is truly contagious. Of course, the great role models I had growing up—my parents, my family—were the first source of inspiration and a constant reminder that when you work hard and smart, you can achieve almost anything. I also always try to surround myself with people from whom I can learn and who are successful in what they are doing. And by being successful, I don't mean just financially. To me, success is when a good balance between your personal and professional life is achieved.

Nina: How much time do you spend networking?

Maria: Not as much as I should, and that is something that I regret and try to improve on.

Nina: For a female who is either starting or rejoining the business world, what advice would you give her?

Maria: Talk to other women who are already where you would want to be. Look for networking opportunities that involve women in business. Be prepared to work hard. Be prepared to make sacrifices. Get as much information about what you want to do as you can before you get into it.

Nina: What has been your greatest obstacle in your career?

Maria: For as much as I prepared myself to be a business owner here, the fact that I didn't grow up in America made it much more difficult for me to penetrate the business world and understand it. That cost me a lot of money, a much slower start, and a harder beginning.

Nina: How did you overcome that obstacle?

Maria: I learned from my mistakes as fast as I could. While this might be true for most people who make mistakes, some of the ones I made were really pertinent to viewing things from my cultural standpoint and not the American one.

Nina: Given a platform to speak to women, is there anything else you would like to say to them?

Maria: Don't let go of your dream. We women make for amazing business owners and are amazing assets to any company. Believe in yourself and look for other women who are in positions similar to the one you want to be in. Women are more supportive of each other and more willing to share and help other women succeed.

Although it wasn't my biggest obstacle when I entered the business world here, I still had a hard time at the beginning dealing professionally with the male environment. I was often not taken too seriously and left waiting for answers. Often, people would ask for "the husband" or the male partner when it came to making decisions about the business, as if being a woman alone growing my business was something so impossible to do. It was surprising to me given that this society is supposedly much more open-minded…maybe it was the '90s. It is not happening today, and that is in part because I am in a different position today as an established businesswoman.

One other important item to keep in mind is the price women pay when it comes to family and relationships. Unfortunately, it is still harder for a woman to grow professionally while maintaining a fulfilling personal life.

A Final Note

Now that you've read this book, what's going to change for you?

Look at all the things we've discussed and you've learned in this book, from looking for a job and interviewing in today's job market, to networking, how to manage up, how to dress for success, how to deal with workplace issues, and how to be professional at all times.

I hope you filled out the exercises honestly and put a lot of thought into them. As you look back at the chapters, I'm sure there are several that really stick out for you, ones with information you need for your current challenges. Now, while all this information is fresh in your head, write a list of all the things you are going to do differently to make your career all it can be.

____

____

____

____

____

____

____

____

Remember to contact me with any and all questions or concerns you have. I would love to hear from you about which chapter(s) meant the most to you and why they helped you. I am also open to coaching you and helping you get to the bottom of any issue you are having. I'm sure there isn't much that I haven't been through, and together, we can put together a plan to get you through it as well. I know you want to succeed, so remember I'm available to help you anytime.

I challenge you to put the information in this book to work for you; I challenge you to step out and to get out of your comfort zone. I challenge you to get out of an uncomfortable working environment if you're in one, and to find a way to make a difference in your workplace and in helping other women.

Thank you for letting me share my experiences, my knowledge, and my life with you. I wish you much success and good luck on your journey. I want you to know I am here to help you, so don't be afraid to ask.

Good luck to you! I wish you all the best and much success.

Your friend always,

Nina Baldwin

About the Author

Nina Baldwin is the chief operations officer for Pallino Restaurants located in the Northwest. Prior to working at Pallino, she was President of Mancha Development Company, which owns and operates seventy restaurants in Southern California and Nevada. She has been in the restaurant business her entire working career. She started in the restaurant industry as a teenager and has worked her way up the ladder, having had the opportunity to experience almost every position along the way.

Given her years of experience, Nina felt there were many insights about the business world she could share so she decided to write *Helping Women Succeed in Business*. Nina hopes the knowledge and advice conveyed in the book will help other women as they climb the corporate ladder or grow and develop in any business they choose. She wants to help women be as successful as they want to be and she is open to coaching or speaking for any organization large or small, including nonprofit groups.

Today, Nina lives in Seattle, Washington. When she is not busy working, Nina enjoys exercising, reading, and when possible, spending time outside enjoying the sunshine. Nina also has a home in Southern California where she visits so she can spend time with family and friends.

Visit Nina at:

www.HelpingWomenSucceedinBusiness.com